D1029772

THE OUTLAWS ON PARNASSUS

Margaret Kennedy

THE OUTLAWS ON PARNASSUS

THE VIKING PRESS: NEW YORK

Library of Congress catalog card number: 60–5838
Printed in the U.S.A. by The Murray Printing Co.

To

John and Gilda Archibald

Thanks and acknowledgements for permission to quote are tendered to: Sir Compton Mackenzie (*The Vanity Girl*); the executors of the late Sir Anthony Hope Hawkins (*The Dolly Dialogues*); the Owners of the Copyright (*The Old Wives' Tale*); Miss Elizabeth Bowen (*A World of Love*); Mr. Leonard Woolf (*The Common Reader* by Virginia Woolf); Dr. E. V. Rieu (translation of *The Odyssey*).

Contents

Foreword

When I first skimmed through the manuscript of *The Outlaws on Parnassus*, I suspected that Miss Kennedy was discussing fiction from a purely English point of view. Most of the novels she cites are English; the principal exceptions are the works of those classical or Continental authors whom the English have adopted as honorary ancestors. Thus, she devotes a chapter to *The Odyssey*, describing it—and proving her case, I think—as the work of the first true novelist. She often discusses Tolstoi, Proust, and Kafka, but except for Henry James she does not even mention the American authors we most admire. On the other hand, she has many fresh things to say about nineteenth-century British novelists, including those whom Americans have practically stopped reading and whom, for that reason, we like to declare unreadable—

sometimes without even sampling their best work.

Scott is the famous example—who in this country now reads *The Heart of Midlothian?*—but Thackeray promises to be as widely neglected here. Either we are uncompromisingly modern as readers or we insist on being edified by Great Books. Of the British novelists whose work falls in the half-century between Dickens and the Bloomsbury group, the only ones we study are Hardy and Conrad; the others are only names and dates to memorize for examinations. Americans are good at passing examinations. We are very good at getting up a subject—nineteenth-century fiction, for example—if it lies in our field of specialization, but comparatively few of us are general readers, and fewer still have the delighted memory of books that used to be called the well-stocked mind. Many of us are good lecturers to an audience, but we are poor conversationalists as compared with the English—let alone the French—and the result is that we seldom master the art of writing conversational prose.

Miss Kennedy is admirably English in these respects and, except for some pertinent memories of Hollywood, she keeps her discussion close to home. In the first paragraph of her book she says, "There are no Chairs of Fiction at our Universities." There is none at Oxford, but an American reader is likely to remember that there are several professors of fiction at Harvard, and a Department of Creative Writing at Stanford, and a School of Writing at the University of Iowa, where a student can earn his master's degree by concocting a novel. "Things are different here," the American will say to himself —but are they different in the sense that we even try to teach the art of storytelling as Miss Kennedy would like to have it taught? For those of any nation who are capable of learning the art, or simply of enjoying it, her book is full of perceptive examples.

In her last chapter she attacks the English critics for being civic-minded rather than fiction-minded. When they praise a novel for being "serious in the best sense," a phrase she detests, often they mean to say that the author is trying to rouse the public conscience or disseminate ideas for improving society. Once again an American reader will feel that the situation here is vastly different. American critics are still reacting against the civic-mindedness of the 1930s, and now the reaction has gone so far that many of them object to any novel that expresses political convictions or tries to present a broad picture of society. The values our critics would like to impose on fiction are sometimes moral, sometimes intellectual (as when they adjure young writers to develop a sense of irony), and sometimes involved with symbolism, allegory, and the demand for "more than one level of meaning." They are seldom fictional, and I think Miss Kennedy would say that the exact nature of the dogmas is less important than the fact that critics are trying to impose them on storytellers. That is her true complaint, as justified here as it is in England.

Not only does *The Outlaws on Parnassus* have a broader application than appears at first glance; it is also more original. Essentially it is a defense of storytelling against all those who refuse to acknowledge that it is an art in itself. I don't know why the art should need defenders, as it does undoubtedly, or why Miss Kennedy should be the first to come forward—or the first for many years—but apparently everyone else in the literary world has been ashamed of liking just a good story. It isn't an adult taste, the others seem to feel; it isn't intellectual or dignified or socially desirable. Even novelists, when they write about their art, are likely to disparage the narrative element—as E. M. Forster does in *Aspects of the Novel*, where he says that the story is a "low atavistic form" on which a good writer should rely as little as possible, his merit lying rather in the comment he has to offer upon the narrated events. As for professional critics, when they praise a novel it is usually (and for three centuries has almost always been) by describing it as something else than a novel: for example, as an object lesson in morals or manners, as a much-needed sermon, as a sweeping social panorama, a searching inquiry into the human psyche, or a recreation of the Orestes myth, but seldom as a story. Miss Kennedy's comment is that a novel can be anything the critics have praised some novels for being, and anything its author is truly impelled to write—even a sermon or a clinical report—but it has to tell a story or it ceases to be a work of fiction. A novel, she says elsewhere, is a conducted tour through the author's particular landscape, and the story is the vehicle that carries the passengers.

Because critics are seldom concerned with narrative in itself, there has been no agreement on the terms used to describe its various features; one man's theme is another man's subject. Even the key word "story" has never been properly defined. In a chapter that attempts to supply some of the missing definitions, Miss Kennedy says that a story is "a pattern of events so narrated as to evoke an intended response." That is completely accurate so far as it goes, but mightn't it be carried a little farther? It seems to me that any true story consists of four elements. One or more *persons* are involved in a particular *situation*, which leads to some sort of *decision*, as a result of which *something is changed*. All these elements are essential, but of course they assume a vast number of forms. Instead of being a person, the central character may be a wild animal, a big fish, or anything else personified—even a storm or a forest fire, as in two of George R. Stewart's novels. Both the situation and the decision may lie in the past, and the direct narrative may deal only with the perception of change; one example among hundreds is Hemingway's story, "Hills Like White Elephants." In naturalistic novels the decisions are made by nature, not by persons, who merely suffer the effects of natural laws. What this means in effect is that nature (or society) becomes the true protagonist. Most important of all the elements is the something that is changed, but again it takes many forms. In novels of sensibility (or of "egocentric perception," to use Miss Kennedy's sharper phrase) there may be no change whatever in the objective situation, but the hero—or more often the heroine—will have achieved a higher degree of consciousness; that is the something changed, without which there would be no story.

The nature of the change, for better or worse, provides the story with a moral, and that is one thing which readers have never ceased to demand. No matter how sophisticated they may be, they still prefer stories with a pattern or design that implies some general scheme of rewards and punishments. Such patterns, Miss Kennedy says, are becoming harder to find, since life more and more appears to be lacking in harmony and order, until people have come to suspect that it is "a chaos of buses running over them for no reason at all"; that is why they prefer art. I don't know whether Miss Kennedy intends to draw the lesson that storytellers are compelled to invent more and more of their own patterns without reference to life; but if that *is* her notion, I should like to demur. Life provides, so it seems to me, an abundance of patterns that satisfy our longing for a sort of moral logic. When people come to feel there is no reward in this world for virtue or sagacity, and no retribution for malice, perhaps that is because they hold strait-laced or excessively personal notions of good and evil. Life cannot be expected to devise a bad end for every erring wife, in accordance with the Motion Picture Code. It does, however, enforce a sort of justice in its patient and blundering way —that is, unless it is so busy punishing a nation for collective folly that it has no time for individuals. At such times the individuals, if they survive, are left to punish or reward themselves, and that is what they usually do. Even accidents are often part of a logical design. Buses don't run over a random segment of the population; they run over people who blindly step in front of them, and that blind step is the result, in many cases, of an inner compulsion.

What I am trying to say is that life is the only inventor of stories, though most of us don't know how to look for them. We lack the patience to wait for the ending that life provides —*vita longa*, *ars brevis*—as well as the interpretative imagination that would enable us to recognize the stories when they were found. The so-called creative imagination is combinatory at best and conventional at worst; the true creator is life itself. So Polonius might say—and would Miss Kennedy agree? Considering her dislike for every sort of aesthetic dogma, I think she would answer that Polonius has a right to his own opinion.

She believes that storytellers are best when they play their ancient role of outlaws on Parnassus. The only general rule she would impose on their outlawry is one that seems to grant them the utmost personal latitude: *What you can do you may do*. But the rule is less permissive than it sounds, and what each novelist can do is limited by his subject, his skill, and by something she calls "the warrant of inner conviction." Where conviction falters, even great novelists have to fabricate whole scenes out of cheesecloth and newspaper clippings—as she thinks Hardy did when recounting the suicide of Jude's children—while lesser but still highly competent writers often send out for characters to the type-casting agencies. Miss Kennedy has a sharp eye for borrowed characters wherever they appear, in high or low fiction. What I most enjoyed in her book was a sureness of discrimination which convinced me, once again, that novelists are the best critics of the novel.

MALCOLM COWLEY

The novel remains still, under the right persuasion, the most independent, most elastic, most prodigious of literary forms.

Henry James

CHAPTER I

The Late Arrival

The status of the novel, as a form of art, has never been clearly determined. No particular Muse was assigned to story-tellers. There are no Chairs of Fiction at our Universities. Criticism has never paid to the novel the degree of attention which it has accorded to other kinds of literature.

From the earliest times men have felt the impulse to tell stories, just as they have felt the impulse to draw bison on the walls of caves, mould clay, sing songs, mime, dance, beat drums, and make little flutes from reeds. From these tribal activities, these folk arts, have sprung achievements which are rated among the major glories of mankind. The descendants of those first votaries are sure of their place; we know what they have been doing. All are established save the story-teller, left behind in the morning of the world, to weave his magic by the tribal fire. A backward, savage creature, he squats at the foot of Parnassus, doing something so primitive that he really cannot be countenanced unless it can be asserted that he is doing something else.

Men may stand enraptured before a Tiepolo or a Monet, they may spend an evening listening to Beethoven, with no further justification than an avowed enjoyment of pictures or music. They may read poetry because they like poetry. It is not claimed for painters, poets, or musicians that they refine our manners, elevate our morals, widen our outlook, awaken our social conscience, teach us history, teach us geography, or supply us with a realistic interpretation of life. Novelists, if commended at all, are always found to be doing something useful in this line, although the kind of good which they do to us, the brand of edification supplied, has varied with the period. Just now, in the middle and late fifties, some flavour of the dispensary is highly esteemed. To describe a novel as 'medicine' is to praise it. The novelist may not have intended to brew medicine; in that case he had better hold his tongue and thank his stars that he is praised at all.

2

The Late Arrival

The chief reason for this ambiguity of status goes back a long way. In the Western world all the other arts had emerged from their infancy, had been duly handed over to the care of their respective Muses or, at least, respectably lodged upon Parnassus, by 500 B.C. The Greeks, at that period, had no novels. Narrative, the story-teller's medium, served the drama and the epic poem, but played a subsidiary part in both.

This was not because the Greeks lacked the wit to write novels but because such an activity would have challenged their idea of dignity. Professor J. S. Phillimore puts it thus:

'Quintilian's oft-quoted sentence allows the Romans a clear superiority over the Greeks in only one form of literature, the *Satira*, the invention of Menippus, a half-Semite, and a thing so irregular and free and subjective that it was forbidden to the Greeks by that instinct which led them in all the greater exhibitions of their art completely to suppress the author in the creation, the actor in the part played. For their great principle, expressed in the very term *mimesis*, insists on the mask and the make believe; but in the *Satira* the poet speaks on his own authority; his value as a man determines the value of his words. . . . It was not so in the noblest masterpieces of Greek: there the

3

poet goes for almost nothing: his poem is impersonally put on trial, to stand its chance by the less or more of beauty or consistency in it. . . . This belongs to the great and lasting Greek "convention of dignity".'*

The arts recognized in that extraordinary period, so short yet so timeless, have been allowed ever since to live by their own laws, to be an end in themselves, to need no justification, hallowed as they were by close ties with religion and by a belief in divine inspiration. Some radiance of that early glory still rests on them. No later achievement of the forgotten savage, the tribal story teller, no *War and Peace*, no *A la Recherche du Temps Perdu*, can compensate for his absence at the first rites.

He climbed the hill too late, when men and gods had parted company. Nothing had ever been said about him by those titans who first minted the language in which we think and talk of art. He claimed the same lineage as his brethren but could not explain why he had not come out of the Bush when they did. Nor could he give a very creditable account of himself over the centuries; the last two hundred and fifty years are all that he can mention with

* *The Greek Romances*, J. S. Phillimore. *English Literature and the Classics.*

complete confidence. Before that he can only point to a few widely scattered masterpieces, from the *Satyricon* to *Don Quixote*, and to a fairly slender collection of museum pieces, of interest only to scholars. How came it that an art, for which he claims so much, should have attracted so few distinguished votaries? Why was it, for the most part, deputed to women and children, and treated as a diversion for ignorant and idle minds? The epic heroes of the Homeric age dwindled into 'he whose tale is told by our looms'. Tales told by looms deteriorate. The heroic gives way to the wondrous incident, the gaping marvel, to floods, fires, pirates, witches, cruel stepmothers, and visits to the moon. Charito and Xenophon of Ephesus give us a glimpse of what was popular in the first and second centuries A.D. (So how did poor Habrokomes escape? Why! The cross to which he was bound blew into the Nile, luckily face upward, and he floated on it comfortably all the way back to Alexandria.)

Puerility is not the only accusation of which this late arrival has had to clear himself. According to Plutarch, the Parthians pretended to be much shocked at the novels found in the luggage of officers in Crassus' army. The name of one is given, *Milesian Tales*, by Aristides of

Miletus. This book was known to Ovid who refers to a translation of it (*Tristia* 11. 413, 443) and there is no doubt that it had much in common with the little French romances which Pepys hoped the Lord would forgive him for reading on a Sunday. It was not until the eighteenth century that the novelist entirely shook off his association with professional pornography.

Yet there was no driving him off. Denied a respectable temple or altar of his own, he hung about the holy hill, a gipsy squatter, pursued his shady calling, discovered and abode by his own laws, never completely discountenanced yet never felt to be quite respectable. The easiest way to deal with him has been to declare that he is, after all, a useful fellow, and that the novel is of some practical value—good for the morals, good for the manners, instructive or medicinal.

There is, in the second place, very little demand for genuine criticism of the novel. Expert advice in this field is not felt to be necessary. It is a very easy kind of book to read. The other arts strike the average man as being much more mysterious, and as making more strenuous demands upon him. When delighted by poetry, music, or painting he is inclined to ask why he should be thus affected. He is aware of some complicated process of statement and response. Endeavouring to understand this experience he turns to critical comment for elucidation. He is less likely to feel all this when he enjoys a novel; that pleasure strikes him as simple, natural, and familiar. He cannot remember a time when he did not enjoy stories; his pleasure has blossomed from very early roots and from the days when his mother used to tell him about *The Three Bears* at bed-time. He has been so long and so well acquainted with this kind of satisfaction that, when he encounters it as an adult in an expanded form, he takes his response for granted, as he did as a child.

Moreover he probably supposes that it is comparatively easy to write a novel. It is a widespread myth that no particular gifts, no special technical mastery, are needed for this kind of art. People will often remark that they could write a marvellous novel upon their own experiences, if only they had the time; they would readily allow that more than time is required for the production of a marvellous picture, a marvellous symphony, or a marvellous sonnet.

7

This myth is not entirely without foundation. It is, in fact, very easy to write something which will look quite like a novel for several years. There is no other art which can be so successfully imitated. Anybody with brains, education, verbal facility, and some powers of observation can produce a very plausible piece of synthetic fiction. He has only to pick one of the basic plots, adopt the narrative form in vogue at the moment, assemble characters which are either portraits of his acquaintance or stock types borrowed from other books, and serve it up with such sauce as his wit may provide. If his wit is exceptional the result may have a good deal of merit. There has always been a number of successful novelists who have done no more than this, and have been quite unaware that there might be anything more to do. Their wit has earned them a temporary reputation, but they begin to date very soon. Time itself makes them unreadable. The wit takes on the faded aspect of a topical *jeu d'esprit*, of a ten years' old dinner-party conversation.

Later generations, reading such novels of this kind as have escaped complete oblivion, are astonished at the esteem in which they were once held. The gulf between the non-artists and the minor artists, of any period, seems to be so much greater than that between the minor and the major artists. Harriet Martineau, Susan Ferrier, Charles Lever, Bulwer Lytton, and Blackmore strike us now as having some kinship with the outstanding writers of their time; they were doing the same sort of thing and doing it less well. What Mallock, Emily Eden, and Disraeli thought that they were doing is not so apparent, although there may still be reasons why they can be read with interest.

Intellect and wit can, for a time, mask the absence of creative power in this one field. They do not get a man very far in any other; indeed, they rather tend to discourage him from attempting any other. They prompt him to suspect that he had better not turn poet or painter without natural aptitude or technical experience. So little has ever been said about the equipment necessary for a novelist that a man of wit and intellect may be pardoned for supposing that none is needed. He merely thinks that he can turn out something quite as good as most of the novels on the shelves at W. H. Smith's library, as, in fact, he probably can.

Finally, there has always been a recognizable note of uncertainty in the way that novelists themselves will talk about their work. It is as though they never feel quite able to say what they are doing. That assault upon dignity, the mere possibility of which prevented the Greeks from envisaging such an art form, is perhaps never quite out of their minds. It may be for this reason that they speak up so faintly in defence of their calling and have often been known to abuse it. Jane Austen complained of this blackleg tendency among her colleagues, and well she might, when so accomplished a writer as Maria Edgeworth could disparage her medium and her readers in such passages as this:

'If among those who may be tempted to peruse my history there should be any mere novel readers, let me advise them to throw the book aside at the commencement of this chapter; for I have no more wonderful incidents to relate, no more changes at nurse, no more sudden turns of fortune.'

Even when the artist does speak up for his art, he has seldom resisted the pressure put on him to describe it as useful, to fall in with the jargon of the day and declare that it is supplying whatever goods are currently in demand. For two and a half centuries novelists have often fallen into a hucksterish tone when commending their wares.

The Late Arrival

'Read a novel, pretty lady! It's more than a novel: it's food! It's serious. It will teach you something. Read an elegant novel and polish up your manners. Read a noble novel and give your morals a treat. Read a nice bit of stark realism: it's your duty to know what goes on in the slums. Take what the doctor ordered. It's better than a novel. It's a cathartic!'

They are uneasy, as their colleagues, in the other arts, are not. That unanswered question: Where can a novelist put himself? haunts him with the fear that the reader, also becoming aware of it, may tell him. From such treatment other artists are safe. They were rescued long ago from a life of sufferance, of dependence upon the patience, the whims, the stupidity of the tribe. They were taken elsewhere and put under the protection of a god. Compared with them the novelist is a busker outside the theatre, a tumbler at the fair. He knows that, whatever he may say he does, he is still, to most of his public, the voice that told about *The Three Bears* at bedtime.

CHAPTER II

The Missing Definitions

It is a great misfortune for any human activity if the Greeks, as was seldom the case, had no word for it. The chances are that it will stagger through the ages shackled by ambiguities, since it never got itself thoroughly defined at the start. The most useful words in which to discuss it are missing, and there is no original debate to which any dispute can be referred.

In a discussion of the drama, for instance, it is always possible to ask what Aristotle meant by irony, pathos, the unities, and the protagonists. Since he never deliberated upon the novel we do not know what meaning he would have attached to a plot or a story save in relation to tragic drama. If he did not define these things, who can? Who should?

The Missing Definitions

Conflicting definitions are shot backwards and forwards, like an everlasting rally on a tennis court. A writer will discover that a colleague, whose pudding he will swallow with extreme relish, has nothing comprehensible to say about the antecedent ingredients and processes. What is steaming to one is baking to the other. His flour is the other cook's sugar. The proof of the pudding is in the eating and the other cook must therefore be talking sense, in some other language. Since no Athenian Mrs. Beeton ever established the language they must remain at loggerheads. Each will continue to speak his own, yet neither will venture to set himself up as the ultimate authority.

THE STORY

In 1927 Mr. E. M. Forster gave his Clark Lectures at Cambridge, later published under the title of *Aspects of the Novel*. He seized this opportunity for a determined effort to disentangle the novel from *The Three Bears* and Habrokomes floating down the Nile. The story, he declared, has no intrinsic aesthetic value; it is merely a structure, a support for 'finer growths'. He defined it as: A narrative of events arranged in their time sequence.

This has never satisfied those who think that

13

some further distinction should be made between a story and a newspaper report on the local School Sports. Both are narratives of events arranged in their time sequence. To these dissenters, on the other side of the tennis net, there must be some art, implicit in narrative, which will shape events into a story. They hold by an alternative definition: A pattern of events so narrated as to evoke an intended response.

A funny story should make us laugh. A sad story should make us cry. If ill told they are neither funny nor sad: they are not stories at all, but the raw material for stories: mere events narrated in their time sequence. Bored listeners complain that they have no point, meaning that they evoke no response.

This emerges very clearly when screenwriters meet in conference to settle the 'story line' for a picture. At one such conference a certain play had to be altered in order to satisfy the requirements of the Hays Office. In this play an unfaithful wife, forgiven by her husband and reconciled to him, settled down in the third act to a serene middle age. The Hays Office insists, or did insist at the time that this picture was made, that any unfaithful wife must come to a bad end in the eighth reel, however wanton her behaviour during the preceding seven. This was stipulated in order that wives in the audience should not be corrupted. The great reconciliation scene could not be dropped, since the entire story led up to it; the conference was called in order to settle the problem of combining it with the necessary bad end. The Director suggested that, after the reconciliation, the wife might go for a walk and be run over by a bus. In this way, he said, her guilt could be expiated and the picture would get past the Hays Office. To the objection that the bus would not run over her because she had been guilty, he replied that this would be an improvement since it would be exactly like real life. A bus does not inquire into our morals before running over us. To be as like life as possible must surely be the chief aim of art?

There is nothing wrong with this, as a narrative of events arranged in their time sequence, but he had everybody against him when he endeavoured to call it a story. The backer, who had turned up, complained that people want art because life is like that—a chaos of buses running over them for no reason at all.

Men ask of the story what they ask of any other kind of art. They want pattern, design, order, and harmony: they want some contradiction, not of the tragedy but of the pointlessness in human existence. They want some token from the Imperial Palace which their imaginations continually suggest to them, whether or not they believe that they came thence, go thither. They may think of it as an Olympus reserved for the gods, or as a Jerusalem promised to the godly, but they describe it in the language of art. There, *there*, they say, all utterance is music, all nature a tended garden with its gallant walks. Order reigns there and there alone. They utter their longing for it in those rearrangements of perception which they call art. The purest art of the Western world was produced by people to whom the stock epithet for humanity was 'wretched' and who looked for no redress in any future existence.

Actual human events are sometimes so obliging as to arrange themselves into a satisfying design, one in which an element of surprise is combined with harmony and order. We are delighted at this; we call it a *true story*, and tell it eagerly. But, the longer we live and the more we see of the prevailing disorder, the fewer the designs which we can whole-heartedly accept. So much, which once pleased us, is now invalidated by experience. It is no more

16

reckoned possible. *And so they were married* does not carry with it the conviction that they *lived happily ever after*. *Once upon a time there were three brothers* does not guarantee that the youngest will turn out to be the cleverest. The fairy tale sheltered our childhood and our first introduction to 'this wilde world', but its spell evaporates. The design in events, the story which will satisfy the adult mind, is rare, and requires some effort of response. This is, perhaps, why a liking for stories is called childish. People with childish minds have a larger choice and are easier to please.

It is possibly some such appeal to the mature which explains the continued popularity of Walter Scott, who is still second only to Dickens in demand at our public libraries. His public is a mystery to those who do not care for him and who are offended by his literary shortcomings. It was bad enough, they feel, that so very raffish a busker should have exerted so enormous an influence in his own day. He was careless and lazy. He wrote for money. His gifts were none of them of the first order. Yet, single handed, he turned the eighteenth-century novel into the nineteenth-century novel.

He found it a domestic, almost a parochial,

17

affair, entirely concerned with men and manners. In this form it reached its perfection with Jane Austen, who died, as Petronius says Myron died, 'without an heir'. All art is governed by the law of *brevis in perfecto mora;* that which is done perfectly is thereafter done no more. Jane Austen had no imitators because she was inimitable. She cannot be said to have exerted any influence over the novel save to leave to all her successors, for ever, an unsurpassed example of conscience and discipline.

Scott, who had little of either, died with many heirs. He rescued the novel by carrying it into the larger world of men and affairs; he made excursions into a territory hitherto unexplored. In his best work, which is always about Scotland, he opens upon many themes and subjects which have occupied novelists ever since. He had scores of imitators and his influence was continental. It is not this fact, however, which gets him readers now, since other writers have since done what he did first, and done it better.

His public now probably approximates to that public which, in his own day, he knew and understood best: ministers suckled on the Shorter Catechism, learned Writers to the Signet, tough old ladies with long memories, living up three pair of stairs in the wynds of Edinburgh.

The Missing Definitions

Such readers do not often care for novels; they find them juvenile. They have no taste for fairy stories nor for the unconscionable clamour with which some people will discover that the world is wild. But they make an exception in favour of *Waverley*, or *The Heart of Midlothian*, or *Old Mortality*.

Few novelists have been less romantic or have made shorter work of love interest. A nice girl, kept in cold storage till the end of the book and awarded to the hero when his part in the great world is over—that is the most which Scott generally concedes to romance. No romantic novelist would have carried the tale of Jeanie Deans beyond the point where she wins a pardon for her sister: few novelists of any sort would have treated its bitter, inevitable end with so little fuss, when that sister, gone up in the world, writes to Jeanie begging for a disclaimer of their relationship and enclosing fifty pounds as a bribe for silence. No spinner of fairy tales would have created a Waverley, dreaming of friends to die for, until he is confronted by one of the lowly, forgotten friends whom he has abandoned to die. Scott wrote for those who have lived long enough to know that others are rather more likely to die for us than we ever are to die for anybody. There are many such readers and stories to satisfy them are not plentiful.

Moreover they like the world in which they find themselves. The story is not the whole content of a novel. It is rather a conducted tour through the author's particular landscape, and the narrative is the vehicle which carries the passengers. Some writers have commanded a world so expansive and diverse that they have offered a great variety of trips; others have offered but one, and have told the same story over and over again. These landscapes range from the snug and homely to the strange and terrifying. In one such cosmos people will look out of the window at the stars and exclaim: 'On such a night as this, I feel as if there could be neither wickedness nor sorrow in the world.' In another, they poke their heads by mistake into a cupboard and inform their astonished cronies that the night is 'hellish dark and smells of cheese'.

Our favourite novelists are those to whom we return for the sake of that landscape, long after the conducted trips have become familiar pathways. In a world which we find commonplace or disagreeable we may take a turn or two, if the tour is well arranged, but we make no home there. No novelists have felt able to turn the reader loose in their private world without arranging a tour of some sort. For most, indeed, such a voyage of discovery is necessary, if they would truly know their own domain. In telling a story they explore its mountains, deserts, frontiers, and rivers. In this terrain will the projected design hold good? Can the intended response be secured? They cannot know until they have tried. They tell stories because they are like Gide's lady who protested: 'How can I know what I think till I see what I say?'

THE PLOT

Writers are also seldom agreed in their definition of a plot. To some it is a piece of ingenious construction in which an author can claim proprietary rights. He can say that somebody has stolen his plot, meaning some unexpected solution to a mystery, some clever feat in mechanism which nobody thought of before. How can the heroine marry the hero when there is a stain upon her birth? It turns out that there is none. She was born in the year that the calendar was changed. By one system of dating her parents were married immediately before her birth, by another, immediately after. So soon as a mathematical mind gets to work on these facts the stain is removed. This would be described by many writers as a plot.

It appears that Virginia Woolf would have been among them. In *A Writer's Diary* she says that she can make up stories but cannot make up plots. This has caused some astonishment to writers who attach a different meaning to the word. One young novelist, hearing of it, exclaimed:

'But how could she say so? Why, her books are *all* plot.'

To people on the other side of the tennis net a plot means a kind of composition line, a rudimentary suggestion of pattern, which governs the whole work. Nor do they believe that any writer need make up a plot unless he likes. There are plenty of them lying about, natural patterns in human events, some of which are so suggestive and compelling that they have been used by novelists again and again.

A plot, in this sense, is quite impersonal and carries no guarantee of merit. A very good or a very bad story can be written on the same plot, just as good and bad pictures may have the same composition line. Many stories, quite different in texture and implication, can be written on an identical plot.

Here is an instance: In a country ruled by an

alien, insensitive, but efficient race, a young man, belonging by birth and education to the oppressors, is driven by humanity and liberal sympathies to take sides with the weak, native oppressed. His own people call him a traitor. His new comrades never quite understand or accept him. By an amazing chance the oppressed score a sudden and unforeseen victory over the oppressors. The advantage is all thrown away because the poor victors are too fanatical, too inexperienced in affairs, to understand the value of compromise. They will not consolidate their gain and make it the basis of a small but sure step forward; they dream of total victory. The hero, trying to put his worldly wisdom, a wisdom learnt among the oppressors, at their disposal, is suspected and rebuffed. He can, after all, do nothing for them.

That is the abstract and at least two well-known novels have been written on it. The scene of one is in Scotland, of the other, in India. The heroes are called Morton and Fielding. The Cameronians unexpectedly defeat Claverhouse. The British case suddenly collapses at the trial of an Indian accused of criminal assault. But nothing comes of either victory and the two young men, turning their backs upon the whole sorry business, do their best to forget it. The energy and common sense which they were unable to instil into their friends stands them in good stead in their personal affairs. They marry nice girls, kept in cold storage for them, and do well in the world. Against a background of unresolved conflict their personal success and contentment strikes an ironic note.

As stories, *Old Mortality* and *A Passage to India* are totally unlike. But they have this striking factor in common, and how can it be described save as a plot? A theme or a subject would be too general a term and would not suggest so compulsive a pattern. Yet nobody could possibly suggest that Mr. Forster stole it from Sir Walter Scott. It does not appear to have been invented by either of them; in certain conditions these patterns inevitably take shape. The world is full of Mortons and Fieldings, who take the part of the persecuted, the victims of injustice, and fail because the persecuted can so seldom be persuaded to look after themselves with the efficiency which seems to come as second nature to the persecutors. Scott did this sort of thing first; his heirs, among whom is Mr. Forster, developed it.

A strong element of irony is characteristic in several famous and often used plots. It is there in all stories written on the line of 'The Dead Wish'. A man's emotional life is shaped by frustrated desire for something ever denied to him. At last the desire dies, and then the fulfilled wish is forced upon him. This is the governing line in *Vanity Fair*. Dobbin marries Amelia after he has ceased to love her. Virginia Woolf uses it in *To the Lighthouse*.

Irony enables the writer to tell the story from a choice of angles. This is particularly the case in a much used plot: that of 'The Stranger in the House'. The safe, rich, happy people take in a waif, a wanderer, a foundling. He repays them by pulling the house down about their ears. This is sometimes told from the point of view of the stranger. Moses and Perseus both ended by destroying the houses which had sheltered them as infants. It is more usual, however, to take the side of the house. In Simone de Beauvoir's *L'Invitée* the lady of the house quietly murders her little protégée just in time, and she has the entire sympathy of the reader. In Elizabeth Bowen's *The Death of the Heart* the damage is mutual; the house is deadly to young Portia, but she brings it into pretty bad shape by the time that she has done with it. The same might be said of Heathcliff and the Earnshaws in *Wuthering Heights*.

The Oedipus plot indicates the history of a man who dreads some particular fate, takes elaborate steps to avoid it, and, with each precaution, unconsciously brings it a little nearer. It is inviting, but tricky to handle, since the climax must be inevitable and not contrived. Yet truth dictates it; there is a dire attraction in anything that we dread. Kylie Tennant has used it lately in *The Joyful Condemned*. A mother, imprisoned for life, makes heartbreaking sacrifices in order that the shadow of the prison shall never fall upon her child. Those very sacrifices lead to the day when she recognizes her daughter, a convict in the same prison.

Not all novels have plots which can be extracted and identified in this way. Writers have differed very much in the importance which they attached to the governing line. Of Henry James it might easily be said that some of his stories are all plot. The names of the characters may not stick in the reader's mind, but the general pattern does. When asked what a James novel is about, a reader will often simply give the abstract blue-print:

'Oh it's about a man from Boston who went

to Paris for a month and never came back. So they sent another man from Boston to fetch him away, and he never came back either.'

When asked what a Dickens novel is about he will say:

'Oh that's the one Mr. Micawber comes into.'

To those writers who set great store by the blue-print it is a matter of amazement that anybody could have written as Dickens, and many of his contemporaries, did. They published in monthly, or even weekly instalments, and were often pressed to get the material in on the deadline date. No book could survive such treatment unless it had a bunch of characters whose names nobody could forget, once they had been encountered. They were the Mrs. Dales, the Archers, of their day. When *Oliver Twist* was appearing, the first boy at Rugby School to get hold of a certain number rushed through the quadrangles screaming: 'He's murdered her! He's murdered her!' Heads appeared at windows. All the school ran out to learn that Bill Sykes had murdered Nancy. Trollope, in his *Autobiography*, described a conversation which he overheard in the Athenaeum Club between two clergymen who were strangers to him. They were complaining that he used the same characters over and over again. 'If I could not

27

invent new characters,' complained one, 'I would not write at all.' They grumbled about the duke, and they grumbled about the arch-deacon; when they began to grumble about Mrs. Proudie Trollope could bear it no longer. He jumped up and exclaimed: 'I will go home and kill her before the week is over.' This he was able to do with perfect ease.

Nothing very subtle in the way of a blue-print would do for this sort of thing. A Dickens novel had to end sometime, whereas a radio serial can go on for ever. A story line of sorts developed from number to number, and, in the last, certain mysteries were cleared up. This is perhaps why mysteries and suspense devices have come to be confused with plots.

There is a particular line which is a little too shapeless to be called a plot, but which can hardly be described as a subject or a theme. Examples of it are to be found most often upon those shelves in the libraries which are labelled *Romance*. Why such a label should have been chosen is mysterious, as the chief patrons of these shelves are elderly ladies who, if offered a book from another kind of shelf, will say suspiciously:

28

The Missing Definitions

'Is it a nice tale? Shall I like it? *Does she get him?*'

Nothing could be less romantic than this. In a genuine romance *he* gets *her* and there are not as many examples of it as might be supposed. A list which could begin with *Daphnis and Chloe, Aucassin and Nicolette, The Sleeping Beauty*, and *Lorna Doone* would not really be a very long one. There is a businesslike element about 'Does She Get Him?' which excludes romance.

The line has a shape of sorts since a certain development is implicit. She must, in some way, vindicate her right to him. A vast number of execrable novels have been written on it, and some great ones. The grounds upon which she vindicates her right are a matter of taste and period. If she is Pamela or Jane Eyre she runs away from him. If she is Anne Elliot she sits at home, unobtrusively deserving him. If she is Ruth, she behaves very well to her mother in law. If she is Britomart or Pretty Polly Oliver, she dresses up as a boy and goes after him. The heroine of one period is a prude or a minx to another, or may even be considered as completely imbecile, which was the Wife of Bath's verdict on patient Griselda.

The authentic irony is there, since the

29

question inevitably raises another: Was he worth it? The answer to this again depends upon taste and period, since the qualities which a woman is supposed to value in a man vary very much, according to age and country.

Sventi Bai, a Deccanese heroine of the seventeenth century, donned male attire and pursued him through twelve kingdoms, each of which was ravaged by some particular dragon or ogre. By wit rather than valour she rid each kingdom in turn of its infliction and was rewarded by the hand of the Rajah's only daughter, together with twelve elephants laden with diamonds, rubies, and pearls. When she caught up with him she presented him with twelve beautiful brides and a gross of elephants. Was he worth it? He proved his mettle by marrying all thirteen at a single bridal.

The position of women, their subjection or freedom, has a strong bearing on the value of this plot. The prettier *she* sits, the harder it is for the author to persuade the reader that it was worth her while to go through so much in order to get so little. *He* must be presented as a very fine fellow indeed, and fine fellows are not easily come by, as every novelist knows. An editor of one of the American glossies complained, some two or three years ago, of a shortage in this kind of story, for which there is an unflagging demand. It needs two characters and, in most of the manuscripts submitted to him, there was but one. The fine fellow had failed to materialize. The magazine was, at that time, importing most of its material from England and other backward countries where women are still a little downtrodden.

Even in backward Europe it is becoming a difficult line to handle. Georges Simenon, not a notably romantic writer, has ventured on it several times. His best-known version is that in *La Marie du Port*, where she makes a fine fellow of him by reuniting him to something which he needs more than he needs a wife: she sends him back to a boat and a sailor's life.

It is this inherent difficulty in contemporary treatment which keeps the *Romance* shelf in the shade. There is nothing intrinsically false about the line, but it now needs gifts of a high order if it is to be handled successfully. Such gifts are always rare and the probability is that a 'Does She Get Him?' will be sad stuff. Success however is not impossible. The Richardson, or the Charlotte Brontë, of the nineteen-fifties may be lurking on these shelves, read only by the old ladies. Should this later come to light it will be a sell for the Mandarins of literature.

One of them, morbidly haunted by fear of a derisive posterity, went so far as to take a quick survey of the *Romance* shelves, in the Spring of 1956, just to make sure. Nothing startling was discovered save a copy of *The Loved One* by Evelyn Waugh.

CHAPTER III

The Mask

The incompatible functions of creation and narrative set for the novelist a problem which has never been perfectly solved. As a creator he wants to hide—to be timeless and nameless. He wants his work to stand by itself. It must convince others of its truth without any intervention from him. Narrative, on the other hand, forces him into the open. It is, it must be, addressed to somebody. He is brought into personal contact with his audience over whom he must cast his spell. The need to be at once personal and impersonal shapes the whole of his technique.

He looks to his narrative to establish an atmosphere of validity. This need not be the kind of validity which depends upon evoking sce.es and characters familiar to the reader. H. G. Wells managed to invest a lunar landscape with astonishing validity. Lewis Carroll's Wonderland is far more actual to many readers than Zola's Lourdes. But, whether he is dealing in fact or fantasy, the author has got, if he can, to manœuvre us into forgetting that he invented all this. He must suggest some warrant for its existence beyond that of his own imagination. He must speak as though it all happened somewhere else, and he is merely telling us about it. He cannot say to the reader:

'I have invented a woman whom I shall call Flora. I have decided that her story shall be a very sad one; she ends by throwing herself over a cliff. You will cry when you hear it.'

He cannot say this, because he is aware of the reader's probable comment, since it is the comment he himself would make:

'Why should I cry over something which never happened, and over a woman who never existed? Simply because *you* have decided to push her over a cliff? You need do no such thing. You can decide that she won a football pool, married happily, and had eight children. Why don't you?'

Sad or happy, Flora's fate must be presented as

inevitable. The narrator declares that he has no choice; he must record what really happened.

He would therefore prefer to say that he knew Flora; that she lived in his home town; that his grandmother told him about her; that she was a historical character; that the singular particulars concerning the fate of the unfortunate Flora were related to him by a fellow passenger on the top of a coach; that the tragical history of the Lady Flora is a new tale lately come out of Navarre, to which the gentles must hearken. By such means he can put upon somebody else the responsibility of stating that Flora existed and that she jumped over a cliff. It is none of his doing. Flora must be presented as a creature of like substance with the narrator and the audience, an independent entity, blown together, as we all are, by the winds of heaven. She comes we know not whence and goes we know not whither.

The reluctance which all writers feel, when it comes to acknowledging creation, is expressed by Cervantes in his rebuke to plagiarists. Nobody, he says, has the right to borrow Don Quixote; but he does not base his claim upon the grounds of imaginative monopoly. He says: 'He and I were born for one another: he to act, and I to relate his doings.' This, in a nutshell, is exactly how a novelist wants the reader to think of his characters. They are his only to that limited extent.

For many centuries entire responsibility for them was easy to evade. The laws of copyright may secure to the author property which is legally his, but they define its origin in an embarrassing way. His claim to Flora rests solely upon the fact that she exists nowhere save in his imagination. In earlier days anybody could steal her from him, but he had wider opportunities for suggesting that she had been born elsewhere. Characters and stories were common property; they were appropriated and told at will. Even if a writer had really invented the whole thing he could always pretend that he had not and could assert that he had got it from somebody else.

Since the establishment of copyright much of this latitude has been lost to him. He can still take characters from history or legend, still pretend that he has got it from somebody else, but he cannot borrow, lock, stock, and barrel, characters created by another novelist. This is a great deprivation to the rank and file who cannot depend, as they once did, upon a few giants to do most of the work for them. The plagiarists who borrowed Don Quixote were spared the trouble of convincing the reader that such a person existed, since Cervantes had already done that for them. Today, Mr. C. S. Forrester could have the law of anybody who wrote a book about Horatio Hornblower.

The borrowing is now less flagrant although, of course, it still goes on. It must go on. Novelists of a stature to create and establish original characters do not come two a penny; those so gifted that they never have to send out for anything, not even a piano tuner or an archbishop, do not come more than once in a blue moon. Charlotte Brontë sent out for Blanche Ingram; that haughty beauty, with her fashionable drawl, had been going for a long time. Many of Trollope's subsidiary young ladies (not those in the foreground) seem to have settled their back hair and tripped in from a dozen other books. Today almost any young woman called Doreen, wherever she turns up, seems to have been fished out of the kitty. If she were not, her author would have spared thirty extra seconds in order to find her another name. A hundred years ago Doreen was less recognizable. An author, needing a duchess for a page or two, would prudently borrow a reliable Duchess-type from other novels, if his own experience did not run to one. In presenting a cottage interior he would draw freely and picturesquely on his imagination. Today he would not care who guesses that he never met a duchess, and will revel in inventing a fantastically improbable dukery. But, should he need a dustman's daughter for a page or two, he will guard the guilty secret that he never met one by borrowing 'our Doreen'.

It is a measure of the power of those who can create that the validity which they secure is so complete as to be available for imitations. Stock characters, conventional though they may become, have all originated in some notable innovation. Crabbe describes them as:

> *. . . creatures borrowed and again conveyed*
> *From book to book,—the shadows of a shade.*

They come into fashion and go out again, but the great models upon which they were founded remain timeless. Richardson's Pamela had many shadows. Her triumph over every attack upon her virtue so convinced readers that innumerable young persons, far less skilfully conducted, were able to tread the same path. They are forgotten. Pamela remains.

Mrs. Gaskell's Miss Mattie was another striking innovation. Until *Cranford* was published old maids were universally believed to be spiteful and ridiculous. The innocence, dignity, and pathos of Miss Mattie struck a new note which was struck again, and again, by vastly inferior writers. Readers, having accepted Miss Mattie, recognized these pseudo-Miss Matties as having some validity, since one met them everywhere.

Harriet Martineau was responsible for another stock character which has only just gone out of fashion. She created an interesting young doctor. Before the publication of *Deerbrook* physicians and surgeons, so nearly akin to barbers, were scarcely gentlemen enough to carry a novel. She produced one who could, and he reappears in novel after novel, throughout the nineteenth century. He is handsome and well connected. His professional integrity is terrific. He is inconveniently outspoken about undrained cottages and thus offends Squire. His young wife misunderstands him and thinks that he might have compromised. Enemies accuse him of vivisection and body-snatching. His practice falls off. But, when curses come home to roost and 'the fever' breaks out, he is vindicated. Squire's only child lies at death's door. The oath to Aesculapius prevails; he crosses the enemy threshold. Sometimes the child dies. Sometimes the doctor dies. Sometimes both die.

Sometimes they all get well again. The wife, whether widowed or not, is brought to heel and so is the community. It took a writer of George Eliot's calibre to venture upon a young doctor (old doctors were always allowed to be mercenary and incompetent), whose professional integrity was not beyond reproach, who signed a death certificate against his own conscience, and who finally succumbed to his wife's preference for rich patients. Lydgate is not the shadow of a shade, but it must be observed that his creator's task was made easier by the fact that Harriet Martineau had already done a little of the work for her.

In novels today the sudden appearance of a very good little priest has sometimes puzzled inexperienced readers. This quiet, chubby fellow, in his worn soutane, was originally minted by G. K. Chesterton, for a pretty frivolous purpose; he is now often imported as a buttress to validity. He is an excellent man, simple yet subtle, humble yet firm as a rock. Nothing shocks him although the circles into which many a writer plunges him can scarcely be to his taste. He is brought in for purposes of comment. He explains what view the Church would take of Flora's predicament, whatever that may be. He gives the reader an impression of immense validity since he is expressing, not his own opinion, not the author's opinion, but the opinion of an established Authority. The author has, of course, checked the doctrine in order to make sure that it is correct. The effect on the reader is to make him feel that so tremendous and long established an affair as the Catholic Church would scarcely trouble itself to have an opinion about Flora if there was really no such person.

This good little priest is more freely used by non-Catholics than by Catholics, who have met more priests and are liable to pause and ask themselves whether they have ever actually met one quite like that. Non-Catholics, having read *Father Brown*, know that there are hundreds like him. So strongly is he printed upon public imagination that it would, just now, be quite difficult for an English novelist to venture on a bad little priest. Ill temper, rapacity, stupidity, ignorance, and bigotry go with corpulence and jowls, or with rangy fanaticism.

The appearance of this stock character in a novel by a reputed agnostic will sometimes cause a little surprise. The author's friends ask anxiously whether he is 'going over'. Why should he suddenly take such an interest in Catholic doctrine? The answer is that the 'psychiatrist, who used at one time to be brought in for the same purpose, has now been worked out. He was never half so attractive or convincing as this pleasant character and the Pope's warrant for Flora is worth a dozen warrants got from Freud. It is, however, a kind of borrowed validity which some writers consider to be forbidden by the Queensberry rules.

A reliance upon stock characters saves an author a vast deal of trouble. He can truthfully say that he never invented them. They are to be met with everywhere. For him, the need to establish validity is not vital. For the author with original characters to present it is essential. He is always seeking for some voice, other than the creator's voice, in which to speak of them. The first thing which he demands from his narrative form is some protective colouring, some camouflage which will enable him to disappear into his own landscape. There have been very few writers, of a calibre to be remembered and quoted, who have not exhibited, in their work, some indication that they are aware of the problem and are seeking a mask.

This is not perhaps because all novelists are aware of it, but because, among ten thousand who are not aware of it, only one survives to be remembered and quoted. For the vast majority this awareness is essential. The writer who lacks it is beautifully free from any nagging doubt as to where to put himself. He has a confidence which gives him a most enviable authority of statement, a liberty of utterance such as is otherwise only enjoyed by small children who command the world's attention with a simple: *Look at me!* Unfortunately, this confidence, unless it is combined with substantial creative gifts, is liable to keep him out of print.

If however this messianic assurance is coupled with other gifts, he enjoys a tremendous advantage. He can startle his colleagues by the things which he is able to do; where they would fear to tread he rushes in and completely secures his object. They admire his virtuosity but cannot quite think of him as one of themselves, since it would appear partly to spring from an attribute not necessarily belonging to an artist. He has some kind of outboard motor, whereas they must contend with oars, sails, wind, and tide. They cannot apply to him the tests which they would apply to one another. When asked what they think of him they are inclined to praise his performance and then to shut up. Their objection is too professional to be generally understood.

Perhaps this is why so many writers are guarded in their comments on D. H. Lawrence. They admire his achievement but he makes them feel uncomfortable. He disconcerts them as a nudist might disconcert a company of the clothed. He does not appear to be frightened by something which has always frightened everybody else. Ought he to be? If he had been, would he have written so well?

It is a question for critics to settle. Mr. Frank O'Connor, in his recent study of the novel, *The Mirror in the Roadway*, speaks entirely as a critic, and from the readers' end of the line. It is a work of assessment and appraisal, and an inquiry into that which distinguishes one novelist from another. He does not concern himself with those problems which all novelists have in common, and in the chapter upon Lawrence he indicates no disconcertment. But, in another passage, after quoting a typical Lawrentian paragraph, Mr. O'Connor gives a sudden cry of protest. He attributes this exclamation to the fact that he is a nineteenth-century liberal; as such, he often disagrees with the attitudes revealed by novelists, and says so, but never with so complete a recoil, never in such unqualified terms. Here he complains of the *tone*—the voice which speaks. He

44

quotes Jane Austen's Mr. Woodhouse: 'That young man is not quite the thing.'

Urbanely put, this expresses the recoil which a nudist can inspire. It is possible that Mr. O'Connor is speaking here, not as a critic, not as a nineteenth-century liberal, but as a fellow writer.

CHAPTER IV

Narrative Forms

One of the most convenient masks which an author can assume is that of his principal character. He can take cover behind his hero, who tells the story in the first person singular, and can announce his own existence with a good deal of assurance, since no man can be supposed to have invented himself.

All narrative forms have their own technical advantages, in addition to their main function of offering cover to the creator. This one is particularly suitable for stories in which the passage of time, and the changes wrought by time, may offer a problem. A time lapse is always a danger point. Unless it is skilfully handled, the reader may feel that the thread is broken and the spell weaker. His journey is being interrupted by tiresome halts, waits, and fresh starts. There is a faltering of interest whenever a time lapse is announced. Flora was a child in Part I, and we found her quite interesting. Now, in Part II we meet her again, grown up, and a different person. We hope that we shall like her as well, and in any case the momentum gained in Part I is largely lost. We feel that we are beginning all over again. If she is telling her own story we are less likely to feel this. In *Jane Eyre* there is a nine-year interval between her first two terms at school and her departure as a governess. We accept her statement, that nothing of importance occurred during these years, more easily than we would have accepted it from Charlotte Brontë, who would, had she been telling the story herself, have been obliged to say: 'Nine years passed and Jane grew up. She was, of course, a little altered, etc., etc.' We are already acquainted with the grown-up Jane, telling the story of her own childhood, and do not feel that a new person is being introduced.

Time, in a story, is not an affair of clocks and calendars. It is an emotional element. It is long or short according to its content. That is what our own experience tells us, whatever the clocks may say. Ten minutes in a dentist's chair

last a long time. Ten hours, spent in certain
company, go like a flash. We return from a
picnic and learn that the bottom has fallen out
of the world. There are telegrams, packings,
trains, hospitals, a funeral. Remembering
that picnic a week later we think it was a hundred years ago, because we have lived through
so much in a week. A couple celebrating their
golden wedding may remember a picnic on
their honeymoon, and feel that it was only
yesterday, because there had been so little
emotional change in fifty years.

The novelist must fall in with this emotional
rhythm and convey it. His time lapses must
coincide with those disappearances of time
which occur in every life, when, looking back,
we can recall very little because the landscape
at that period seemed changeless. This effect is
most naturally secured by a person speaking for
himself as his memory dictates. The natural
censorship and selection of that memory seems
less arbitrary than a choice made by an author
telling about him.

It is however a form which can only be used
for a certain type of character; he must be
articulate, clear-headed, and able to give a connected account of things. These are not common characteristics. Not many people could

really sit down and tell the story of their lives, although most believe that they could. Some of the most renowned characters in fiction could not have strung three words together to explain how it all happened. Emma Bovary could not have done so. Henchard could never have explained how he came to sell his wife and why he was Mayor of Casterbridge. Stendhal's Fabrice, the first Great Incompetent, ancestor of a long line of Lucky Jims, could not have explained how he came to be galloping about the field of Waterloo all day, looking for a battle in which he yearned to fight, if only he could locate it.

Prevost, fired with admiration for *Moll Flanders*, embarked upon a version of his own. That he intended to do this quite openly is clear, since he gave his book the same title: *Manon* is the nearest French equivalent for Moll, and *Lescaut* (the Scheldt) the contemporary term for Flanders. He could not take over Defoe's form, even if he had wished to do so, since his Manon was destined to die in the Plantations whereas Moll came back from her sojourn in very good shape, in spite of having married her brother by mistake while there. Manon moreover was never a very clear-headed or sensible young woman, unlike Moll,

49

whose silliest action was to steal a horse when she had nowhere to put it. Manon's story, therefore, had to be handed over to des Grieux.

The power of connected narrative is essential, but the character need not necessarily understand his own story as the reader does. Considerable irony can be achieved if he does not; John Marquand uses this form for such a purpose in *H. M. Pulham Esq.* in which the hero is too much of a gentleman to see that his best friend is a cad, although the reader perceives it. It can also be used for a story which may have two interpretations, as in *The Turn of the Screw*, where the facts retailed by the governess quite warrant the conclusion that she had seen no ghosts but had gone mad. Henry James here relies a little too much upon the imagination of the reader, who is supposed to fill in, for himself, the 'horrors' which the two children discuss when alone together; he is not likely to have read the *procés verbal* upon which the story was founded, and his utmost notion of horror may therefore fall ludicrously short of the mark. He does not know all that he ought in order to make a decision.

A drawback to the use of this form is an element of egotism suggested by a character who talks about himself at such length. This is least likely to be troublesome in an adventure story where he has little to say about his own character, thoughts, and emotions, and is occupied with fires, floods, and narrow escapes. Such a narrator does not have to convince us that he is wise, virtuous, and amiable, and he has a perfectly good excuse for telling his story if his adventures warrant it. Indeed, his validity is increased if he can admit to a certain amount of folly. John Buchan's Richard Hannay, for instance, is at his most convincing when he informs us that: 'Then I did a dashed silly thing.' We are not so ready to like a hero who talks for long about his personal relationships or his emotional experiences; it is not an easy treatment for a very pleasant character. Few readers admire Pamela quite as much as Richardson would have wished, or like her as much as she likes herself. That it can be done, however, is proved by *David Copperfield*, who manages to present himself in a pleasant light without undue complacency.

It is, on the other hand, an excellent treatment for disagreeable or disreputable characters, since it shows us how they see themselves, which is seldom how anybody else sees them. That they often regard themselves as quite good fellows is a truth which nobody else

51

perhaps could convey quite so well. Richard Hull uses this form for this purpose in *The Murder of my Aunt*. Joyce Cary's Sara Monday, in *Herself Surprised*, gives a self-portrait which would not probably have been endorsed by anybody else in the book, or by us, had we met her. Thackeray's *Barry Lyndon* never appears to know what a swine he is, yet flashes into extreme validity when occasionally, amidst his scandalous memories, he comes upon one which he cannot bear to recall. These deeds, which really fill him with remorse, are not his alone; he has shared them with others, to outward view more respectable than himself. At the memory of a farm sacked and burnt by troops during the war he flinches and falls silent. Both Barry Lyndon and Sara Monday tells us things about themselves which no narrator could have told of them half so well.

Finally there is the occasion for such a narrative; it is a problem which troubles contemporary writers more than it did their predecessors. Why does the man tell all this and to whom does he tell it? The most obvious excuse is that of the grand old man, the John Ridd, who has been asked by his descendants to set down some account of those stirring events of his youth, perhaps in the hope that the old bore will shut up about it for a while if he is kept busy writing a book. But not all these autobiographical heroes have got descendants; sometimes their object, in telling the tale, is to explain why they have not. This sudden garrulity is now generally explained by some indication of cause or setting. Characters no longer suddenly, at some unspecified moment in their lives, unbare their inmost souls to *Reader*, as does Jane Eyre. The suggestion is rather that they are telling the story over to themselves. Sara Monday embarks upon her tale with the aplomb of an old party in the bar snuggery who will tell all this to anyone, whether they listen or not. Some incident, some souvenir of the past, will throw the narrator into a long mood of reverie and recollection. He braces himself to undertake a task which he has hitherto shirked. He reviews the whole story from beginning to end, in order to decide, perhaps for the first time, what really happened. Long ago doings at Brideshead might never have been chronicled had not the house been revisited as a billet during the war. The discovery of a lost diary has the same effect upon Leo, in L. P. Hartley's *The Go Between*. This makes some concession to likelihood, but in no case can the 'I' story be called a realistic treatment. Nobody ever remembered so much, so clearly, and in such detail, as these heroes and heroines do.

The story told entirely in letters and diaries, a form popular in the eighteenth century, retains some of the advantages of autobiography and avoids some of the pitfalls. It also allows the characters to announce themselves and saves the author the risk of stating that they exist. It is rather more realistic. There is no doubt about the occasion for these communications. Letters are written for obvious reasons to particular people. It has an added suspense value; it can give day-to-day bulletins of a drama in which the issue is still undetermined, and does not deal in events which are all in the past. The hero who tells his own story must, at least, have survived to tell it. A letter-writer could die; the most famous of them, Clarissa, did die. Yet, as a form, it is not satisfactory since it limits character to a tiny range—not merely to the articulate but to the literate and the infinitely leisured. The heroines of Richardson and Burney only left their writing desks for very short intervals, in order that something else might happen to them. As soon as they had gathered fresh provender for their pens, back they rushed.

As a form it seems least artificial in French novels of the Ancien Régime. In England, even in the eighteenth century, few women, and fewer men, had quite so much time for writing. Saint Preux, in Rousseau's *La Nouvelle Héloïse*, without a profession, without civic duties, with no Bench on which to sit, no fox to hunt, exiled from Paris and therefore unable even to talk, might conceivably pour out his soul upon paper and pour it out for eighteen hours a day. Milord Edouard Bomston, his straitlaced English friend, had not so much time for it. The letter in which Bomston offers the loan of a Château on the Ouse, if only Saint Preux will make an honest woman of Julie, is almost terse compared with those in which they explain to him that matrimony is against their principles. It is, quite possibly, not unlike the kind of letter which Rousseau and his friends were in the habit of writing to one another.

The novel in this form had a short life and was soon dropped. Few attempts have been made to revive it. Letters, used singly or in batches, are still extremely useful, retaining as they do so many of the advantages of autobiography. They can cover time lapses and preserve continuity in a narrative which might otherwise have been brought to a halt. They can reveal and betray the writer. They can announce the existence of characters and set a scene. They do all this without once forcing the author to poke his head up or seem to be telling us anything. Pitt Crawley and the whole Crawley family are first introduced in Becky Sharp's letters to Amelia. Mr. E. M. Forster opens *Howards End* with some letters from Helen Schlegel to her sister which set the scene, announce the existence of these two families, the Schlegels and the Wilcoxes, and hint at the coming clash. As an aid to narrative letters are not likely to be dropped, although they are becoming less effective in an age which communicates by telephone.

The Fictitious Narrator, a character introduced for the purpose of telling the story, might seem at first glance to be an ideal mask. Yet it has not been widely used. Such a narrator has a way of intruding a little too much between the reader and the story. He offers too many comments, and develops too many foibles of his own. Not many writers have kept this character as much in the background as

Mrs. Gaskell did in *Cranford*; we know nothing of the 'Miss Mary' who tells the story save that she has a father. Conrad's Captain Marlow is more typical. He sometimes seems to imagine that his comments are more important than the tale he is telling. Those pauses on tropical verandas, when Marlow for an instant stops talking, are dangerous. The cigars of the listeners glow like fireflies in the night. After a while somebody asks Marlow to go on; the hiatus has given the reader an opportunity to wonder why. There is always the chance that the fictitious narrator may spoil a good story by becoming a bore. He is at his best perhaps when he gives continuity to a collection of anecdotal short stories. A racy character, with an idiom, wit, and style of his own, has been of service to several writers who knew their business. Kipling and W. W. Jacobs maintained a staff of several.

The most interesting use of this form is that made by Emily Brontë in *Wuthering Heights*. She has two narrators. The greater part of the book consists of Mr. Lockwood's account of Ellen Dean's account of events long ago. This double account includes some exquisitely worded prose poetry from Catherine Earnshaw which would have been sadly marred if they had not managed, between them, to remember and record every syllable of it. Many explanations have been offered for this peculiar technical choice. The answer is implicit in the nature of the material to be narrated. It is a story on two time levels which must be treated simultaneously—never allowed to be thought of as *then* and *now*. The gulf between them must be abolished. Ellen Dean is in *then*, in those earlier happenings. Lockwood, a little in love with the younger Catherine, and curious to know how she came to Wuthering Heights, is in *now*, where the consummation of this extraordinary story is to be reached. In this way the young Heathcliff and the lost Cathy hold the scene as though there had been no eighteen-year gap between Cathy's death and the moment of telling. She does not, at any moment in the book, seem to be dead.

It is a unique book, a solitary raid into the border land between the novel and poetry, a foray to its very frontiers. A unique vehicle was needed for the excursion. Emily Brontë chose one which provided her, incidentally, with a double mask; the effect of this is to give her an almost classical anonymity. It is not surprising that her authorship should, in some quarters, be questioned. Had there been no legend of a

scapegrace brother, with a hat full of manuscripts, this doubt might still have arisen. When
a creative miracle is most apparent it is often
thus explained. 'She could not have invented
this' is interpreted as '*She* could not have invented this'. Incredulity of this kind has
occurred in other cases of superb *mimesis*.
Homer could not have invented this! We can
believe it better of a syndicate of archaic poets,
working at different dates and without consul-
tation. Shakespeare could not have invented
this! We can believe it better of Bacon, Mar-
lowe, Essex, Queen Elizabeth, or one of the
drawers at the Mermaid.

The great resource of authors who wished to
narrate in person has been to adopt the convention of the Author-Observer. They boldly
bring themselves on to the stage, but suggest
that they do not know everything, that they
were somehow among those present and are
merely relating what they observed or guessed.
Fielding, for instance, will say: 'I never could
discover that Parson Adams earned more than
£50 per annum,' as though it was not in his
power to bestow upon Parson Adams any income he should think fit. It was a very popular

59

form all through the nineteenth century. The author was an obscure citizen of Middlemarch or Barchester. Trollope could 'never endure to shake hands with Mr. Slope'. Thackeray was an unseen guest at Lord Steyne's parties. Dickens, prowling round London, chanced to look in at the *Old Curiosity Shop*. Flaubert went to school with Charles Bovary. In this way, characters can be introduced, and the stage set, without forcing the author to admit that he made it all up. He is an observer merely.

He can also use it for the purpose of comment. At intervals, after disappearing from the stage for a long time, he pops up again, button-holes the reader, and has a confidential chat about it all. 'I suppose,' he says, 'that you think Flora was behaving very badly? But I don't myself believe that she meant to tell a lie. I think she had convinced herself, just then, that she spoke the truth.'

It is, of course, extremely artificial. The Author-Observer tells of scenes which occurred when he was not present, and of things which no onlooker could possibly have known. It is a solution, merely, of the unsolved problem; it offers a safe place in which the novelist may put himself, and allows him to make some pretence of disclaiming creation whilst giving him

60

a wide latitude in narrative. In a modified form it can still be used. Mr. Somerset Maugham has combined it, several times, with the Fictitious Narrator, in a technique of which Kipling was fond. Many Maugham stories are presented like this:

'I, Maugham, first met Flora in the Malay States. I observed that she looked thin and wretched. Ten years later I met her again. She looked plump and prosperous. I got her story eventually out of her nearest neighbour, a garrulous planter, who, over a sundowner, gave me his reasons for supposing that she had, in the interval, murdered her husband.'

This technique secures a surprising degree of validity. There seem to be many people in the world who are ready to swear that Mr. Maugham invents nothing. All his stories about Flora are perfectly true. Their husband's cousin's wife's aunt lived in the Malay States for years and knew Flora intimately. The double mask carries instant conviction. There is no surer proof of a writer's technique than the assertion, on the part of his readers, that he has no imagination at all, and that everything he says is 'perfectly true'.

The Author-Observer lingered on for some time after he had been officially outmoded. He has a way of cropping up suddenly in the work of writers who, in theory, do without him, but who find themselves obliged to call him in at a crisis, when they have something to relate for which they particularly wish to disclaim responsibility. He is an indication of nervousness. When a character has to be killed he will sometimes edge on to the scene, for this is a task which alarms any experienced writer. The reader will call it wilful murder unless he is convinced that Flora had to die. It is a point at which every support for validity must be summoned, and the author will betray his nervousness in one way or another. He refers to destiny, or puts all the blame for the occurrence on to 'The President of the Immortals'. Arnold Bennett sought safety in a wealth of clinical symptoms; his characters die of old age or of indubitably fatal diseases, from which they could not possibly recover. As a rule he stuck to direct impersonal narrative but on one occasion, when obliged to kill a character suddenly in the prime of life, he pops up in person, as though he were a mourner at the funeral, and says:

'I have often laughed at Samuel Povey. But I liked and respected him. He was a very honest man. I have always been glad to think that, at the end of his life, destiny took hold of him and displayed, to the observant, the vein of greatness which runs through every soul without exception. He embraced a cause, lost it, and died of it.'

This is the Author-Observer at his most robust. 'Povey acted, and I relate his doings. Destiny killed him, not I, and I am glad to be able to observe that he had a vein of greatness. I did not bestow this attribute upon him, as a cook might ice a cake. It is my opinion that a vein of greatness runs through every soul without exception.'

Thackeray, Trollope, and Fielding never dodged responsibility with greater determination.

These narrative forms are all alternatives to direct impersonal statement. There are several others, and more will doubtless be devised. A story can be told almost entirely by the characters in conversation, narrative being reduced to a mere indication as to which of them is speaking.

'I have made a discovery lately.'

'What are you two talking about?' called Archie.

'You are not meant to hear,' said Dolly, without turning round.

63

'Yet, if it is a discovery, he ought to hear it.'

'He has made a good many lately . . . What is the discovery?'

'The discovery is that I am growing middle-aged.'

'You are middle-aged,' said Dolly, spearing her hat with its long pin.

'So will you be soon.'

'Not soon.'

'Some day.'

After a pause Dolly said: 'I suppose so.'

She rose and stood by the sundial.

'What do the mottoes mean?' she asked.

There were two. They looked at life from different points of view.

'*Pereunt et imputanter.*'

'Well, what is that, Mr. Carter?'

'What does it matter? Let us try the other.'

'The other is longer.'

'And better. *Horas non numero nisi serenas.*'

'And what is that?'

'Stop! You will set it moving . . . Freely rendered it means: I live only when you . . .'

'By Jove!' remarked Archie, 'there was a lot of rain last night. I've just measured it in the gauge.'

'Some people measure everything. It is a detestable habit.'

64

'Archie, what does *Pereunt et imputanter* mean?'

'Eh? Oh, I see. Oh, well, you know, I suppose it means you have got to pay for your fun, doesn't it?'

'Oh, is that all? I was afraid it was something horrid. Why did you frighten me, Mr. Carter?'

'I think it is rather horrid.'

'Why, it isn't even true.'

'You are right. If it said that, it would not be true. But Archie translated wrong.'

'Well, you have a shot,' suggested Archie.

'The oysters are eaten and put down in the bill. You will observe, Archie, that it does not say in whose bill.'

'Ah!' said Dolly.

'Somebody has got to pay,' persisted Archie.

'Oh yes, somebody,' laughed Dolly.

'I suppose the chap that has the fun . . .'

'It is not always a chap,' observed Dolly.

'Well, then, the individual. I suppose he would have to pay.'

'It does not say so.'

This extract, read aloud to an audience unacquainted with the source, was unanimously attributed to Miss Ivy Compton-Burnett. The ninety-ish flavour of the dialogue settled the verdict, although it was agreed that the passage was by no means typical. *Nobody else*, declared the jury, could have written it.

The Dolly Dialogues, * from which it is taken, was published in 1894. Anthony Hope's reputation as a successful popular writer should not obscure the fact that he made an indubitable contribution to form. Successful popular writers have often done this, especially those sophisticated enough to attach no great importance to their subject-matter. They have explored new ground which their more ambitious successors have been glad to take over. This is the way in which one author generally influences another. A man's subject-matter is, or ought to be, his own. He cannot take that over from anybody.

It is perhaps for this reason that Mr. J. M. Mitchell, in the preface to his translation of the *Satyricon*, suggests that Petronius would have made an ideal translation of *The Dolly Dialogues*, adding that Petronius was 'the most sophisticated of all the Romans who wrote'. Technically Petronius has been a model

* It must be stated that there have been a few cuts and that an occasional 'I said' from Mr. Carter has been omitted.

66

for many writers by no means as sophisticated as he was, including Smollett and Aldous Huxley. He 'died with heirs' and so, apparently, did Anthony Hope.

Wreaths are not always laid upon the tombs of these explorers. The novel, unlike any other form of art, is always discussed and judged upon content and subject-matter. Yet these can never be fully assessed unless some serious attention is paid to form, method, medium, and process. The whole of what a man has to say will not be perfectly understood by those who do not ask how he says it.

Weekly reviewers, who must pass an immediate judgement on books as they come out, cannot naturally give much attention to technical points, although it does them no harm to know something about method. They are not concerned with the whole of what any writer has to say; it is their business to decide whether any of it is, for any reason, likely to be worth the reader's attention. Academic criticism, considered judgements on the classics and on books which have been thought to deserve a second reading, do undertake to consider the whole content; from them some technical cognizance might be expected.

Sir Desmond MacCarthy, in an essay on *Moll*

Flanders,* suggests that Defoe possessed 'no imagination whatever' and was incapable of 'doing anything but leave facts to speak for themselves'. Using strong phrases about Moll's repentance, 'he does not attempt to make them real to us'. Moll's 'governess', a bawd, a fence, a baby farmer, and an abortionist, appears to be an amiable woman, 'nor can one distinguish, except by their actions, Moll's bad husbands from her good ones'. The form is completely disregarded. It is Moll *herself* who uses these strong phrases; there is no reason to suppose that she knew the meaning of the word repentance. The prudent creature was anxious to make some provision for herself in the next world, in case there should turn out to be one. She had been told that some strong expressions of regret might stand her in good stead, and strong expressions were duly forthcoming. Had it been Defoe's object to tell us which of her gentlemen were good, which bad, he would hardly have left the story in her hands, since she was the last person to know. She happened to be fond of her rascally old governess. Defoe's object was to show us Moll, her gentlemen, her governess and her world, as she saw them.

A painting is not judged solely on its subject,

* *Criticism*, Desmond MacCarthy.

68

by people who have not troubled to observe whether it is in oils or water colour. Of a painter, of any artist, it is simply asked: What was his object? How far did he achieve it? Full cognizance of technical process is necessary for a complete answer. The technique chosen is a guide to the object. When so accomplished and experienced a critic as Desmond MacCarthy withheld from the novel the kind of scrutiny which he would have given to any form of art, the inference is obvious. He did not think it art. Many people do not.

Defoe's 'beautiful bare narrative', as Lamb terms it, does not please all tastes. To some minds the purely factual account of what was said and done demands either too little or too much of the reader. They like comment from the author; they like to be told what to think. To others, much comment from the author often appears to be a dig in the ribs to the simple, in case they might miss a point which, to the subtle, is already abundantly clear. To them the most admired author is he who can abstain from comment yet leave the widest possible range and variety of response to his readers—can be read in one way by the simple, in another by the subtle, and is perfectly intelligible to all. Defoe's art might not, in any case, have been Sir Desmond's cup of tea, but a scrutiny of the purposes, advantages and limitations of the autobiographical form might have made Defoe's object clearer to him.

Defoe, in this case, is partly to blame. He wrote a sadly hucksterish foreword to *Moll Flanders* in which he asserted that it was a very moral story and likely to do everybody a great deal of good. This must have misled Sir Desmond. It must however be remembered that in 1719, when Defoe took to writing novels, the reproach of *Milesian Tales*, and of little French Romances, was still a considerable embarrassment to a novelist, especially to one with this particular story to tell.

CHAPTER V

The Language of Thought

Direct narrative is seldom, when closely examined, as abstract and impersonal as it appears to be. Every scene, everything that occurs, must presumably have been seen, heard, and felt by somebody. The author turns out to be using this or that mind, from amongst his cast of characters, upon which to take the record.

Tolstoi was the great exponent of this technique. He presents each moment as it was perceived by one particular person in an enormous cast, switching deftly from mind to mind so that each contributes a quota to a whole which is only clear to the reader. He uses this method in all his best work. When he abandons it, as in *The Kreutzer Sonata*, for the autobiographical form, the ferocity of his didacticism becomes apparent. There is no check upon it once he has taken cover behind a single character into whose mouth he can put the whole of his comment. In all the novels it is there, lurking in the background, breaking out occasionally, but the discipline of that technique which he employs so superbly keeps it within bounds. He relies on a hundred minds and he cannot force a hundred minds to think and feel as he does.

So subtle and imperceptible are the switches that it is sometimes only by the use of a single word that we know whose eyes, ears, and mind are, at a particular moment, in charge of things. Very often we have the impression that the prospect was common property and belonged to nobody in particular. On studying the passage closely we may locate it as recorded for us by one person present; to anybody else it would not have been quite the same prospect. We get an effect of humanity surveying the scene because such an enormous cast is used. We slide in and out of the minds of all of them, including the most insignificant chance comers.

When Karenin goes to consult a lawyer about a divorce the scene is at first recorded by him. We enter the room with him, share his immediate dislike of the lawyer, and his surprise at a strange gesture made by this man as soon as they are solemnly seated on either side of a desk. The lawyer has caught a moth, and Karenin stares at him with wondering eyes, unable to establish the connexion with the important business which has brought him here. Half-way through the chapter we have gone over to the lawyer. He is staring at his client's feet and trying not to laugh. Another moth flits past. He lifts his hand to catch it but refrains, for fear of hurting Karenin's feelings. A distracting anxiety over his rep curtains is gaining on him. He manages to catch a moth unobserved. As he bows Karenin out he is deciding to have his furniture covered with velvet next winter.

The futility and discomfort of this interview have much to do with Karenin's subsequent refusal to consider a divorce. Between them, each isolated in his separate existence, the two men have taken the story a step forward. Neither, alone, has recorded the whole episode. Had Karenin been capable of perceiving that the lawyer's mind was entirely absorbed by moths, Karenin would have been a different man; he might not have been the sort of man who needs a divorce. The switch from one mind to the other is so adroit that it is only detectable on a careful reading. The reader feels that he knows all that occurred, and is scarcely conscious of the means by which this knowledge has been conveyed to him.

There are a few occasions when Tolstoi abandons this method for a factual account of what was done and said, as recorded by no mind in particular. The effect is horrifying, since it suggests that no mind present was sufficiently humane, at that moment, to take a record—that nobody acting or speaking dared either to think or to feel. This is the effect produced at the party in Dolohov's quarters on the night of the attempted abduction of Natasha. It reaches its climax when Anatole, just before setting off, insists upon the observance of an old Russian custom. All must sit for a moment in silent reflection before a traveller departs on his journey. The worst feelings, the most shocking thoughts, would have been less dire than the emptiness of this moment.

Few novelists use so large a cast as Tolstoi did. It is more usual to rely on the perceptions of two or three leading characters, giving to each a fairly long innings at a time. Sometimes the whole story is confined to the perceptions of a single person; nothing is recorded which has not been heard, seen, felt, and understood by

74

that central entity. There can, on the other hand, be a central character into whose mind we never penetrate, but who is observed by all the others in turn. This is the method adopted by Henry James in *What Maisie Knew*. There has been a recent example of it in Iris Murdoch's *The Flight from the Enchanter*.

So complete a dependence upon a variety of minds, eyes, and ears led writers, who preferred this technique, into a closer study of the actual language of thought. They felt that they ought to convey, with some suggestion of accuracy, that repetitious hurly-burly of emotion, sensation, discovery, astonishment, recollection, debate, indecision, conclusion, self-defence, tirade, and ejaculation which we describe as thinking. Some felt this more strongly than others, but, by 1900, it was not very possible for any writer to convey the thoughts of a man stricken with remorse in terms like these:

'Yes, I have indeed acted towards you with thoughtless cruelty. I brought you from your paternal fields and the protection of a generous and kind landlord, and when I had subjected you to all the rigours of military discipline, I shunned to bear my share of the burden, and wandered away from the duties I had

75

undertaken, leaving alike those whom it was my business to protect, and my own reputation, to suffer under the artifices of villainy. O, indolence and indecision of mind, if not in yourselves vices, to how much exquisite misery and mischief do you not frequently prepare the way.'

He might reach this conclusion, but not by such a short route or in such elegantly turned phrases. In a confused agony of perception his strongest impressions would be visual and auditory. He would hear again and again the whispered reproach. He would continually meet a wordless glance which will, he fears, haunt him till he finally encounters it at Compt. He would see rather than name the paternal fields where his victim once whistled happily at the plough. He would reach his final conclusion only after repeated and horrified assertions that he is not callous, not perfidious, and that indolence, indecision of mind, are not, surely vices?

Scott, when he wrote this passage, would not have maintained that it was an accurate transcription of thought. He had taken some trouble to convey the state of mind. The soliloquy is addressed to the victim, which is obviously right. We are told that the dying

man's whisper rang continually, like a knell:
'Ah Squire! Why did you leave us?' The
paternal fields have been identified as a boy-
hood memory for both of them, and a picture
conjured up of a cottage and bereaved friends:
'old Job Houghton and his dame' to whom the
penitent has promised to be kind if he ever gets
home. In 1814 no novelist would have thought
it necessary or possible to do more. Few would
have done as much.

By 1914 it was felt to be necessary, and
possibilities were therefore explored. Writers
using an orchestra of minds to tell their story
for them were obliged to consider, not only the
exact language of the mind, but the variety
of language, as used by different minds. A
technical device developed which has sometimes been called 'interior monologue'. It is
a soliloquy purporting to be bounded entirely
by the thinker's character, idiom, vocabulary
and range of expression.

As a device it bristles with problems. How
far, for instance, should accent be indicated?
Must the thoughts of a cockney be transcribed
with dropped aitches, and must a place be
called a plice? His accent may play an important
part in his perception. The taxi-driver who
believes that he has been told to drive to the

Avy Restaurant, and who fails to identify this with the Oivy, will not remember the ensuing altercation in quite the same way as does his fare, who thought that he was asking for the Ivy. Nor is the idiom of other people always recorded quite accurately in our recollections. The carpenter who said that Her Grace's very words had been: 'Don't you put nothing down on this here little Cain and Abel. It's Looey-cans,' was probably speaking in perfect good faith.

Many writers reserve interior monologue for the final passage in some train of thought, since very long spells of it are often tiresome. They will keep it in their own hands in the earlier stages, using their own larger vocabulary and range of expression, until some conclusion is reached, when they will pass into the thinker's idiom and let him sum the whole thing up in his own words.

'Was there after all so much to be afraid of in her father? Was not this tradition of his fierceness sedulously maintained by her mother for her own protection? When she looked back at the past, Norah could see plainly enough how all these years the mother had hoodwinked her children into respecting the head of the family. . . . The romantic devotion their

78

mother exacted for him might have been accorded to a parent who resembled George Alexander or Lewis Waller. But as he was only moderately tall for a man (he was the same height as herself), fussy (the daily paper must remain folded all day while he was at the office so that he could be helped first to the news as he was helped first to everything else), mean (how could she possibly dress herself on an allowance of £6 5s. a quarter?)—such a parent was not entitled to dispose of his daughter: a daughter was not a newspaper to be kept folded up for his gratification.

' "For I *am* beautiful," she assured her reflection. "It's not conceit on my part. Even my girl friends admit that I'm beautiful—yes, beautiful, not just pretty. Father ought to be jolly grateful to have such a beautiful daughter. I'm sure *he* has no right to expect beautiful children." '*

Others adopt a style in which the idiom of both is combined. Some phrase, characteristic of the thinker, is introduced now and then, in order to give a kind of local colour to the whole. Flora, buying dress material, might be described as a pilgrim to Samarkand, hovering dazzled between exotic brocades and translucent

* *The Vanity Girl*, Compton Mackenzie.

79

gauzes and settling finally for a shantung which was ever so pretty and wouldn't run.

Neither solution is quite satisfactory, but a completely accurate transcription of thought would be so obscure and complicated that the reader would make nothing of it without a host of footnotes. A purely intellectual process is rare, fatiguing and seldom sustained for long. Nor is it likely to provide much material for a novelist. If a man thinks at all, follows a train of reasoning to its conclusion, puts to himself all the arguments on either side, he will probably have been driven to do so by that activity which occupies most of his waking hours—his profession. He is most likely to think connectedly when he is deciding whether or not to operate, whether to sell out of rubber, or which fields to put into plough. These deliberations do not often bring grist to the novelist's mill. In the business of life, which interests him more, we are all amateurs.

Some kind of rough soliloquy may go on in our heads, but it is a hotch-potch of allusions, associations, memories, half-finished sentences, and echoes from other voices. Nor do we often talk to ourselves. We generally address Another, a protean creature, that *non-ego* which might be held as equally essential to cogitation as is

80

the Cartesian *ego*. We define the intolerable by informing somebody that we will stand no more of it. We defend ourselves against a faceless accuser. We tell the mentors of our youth exactly how wrong they were. The monologue is shaped, the very terms and language used, are determined by the person uppermost in our minds while we think.

Interior monologue can only be a symbol of all this. More was at one time expected of it than it could ever supply. Its use was taken to indicate sensibility and perception in the writer. Now, having seen what can be made of it by writers who lack both, having scanned its limitations, we are perhaps less irritated by Waverley's stilted musings than we might have been fifty years ago. In another fifty years this convention may come in for the same derisive abuse which has, until recently, been bestowed on Scott and his contemporaries by people too blinkered to understand any convention save their own. Their abuse will be ill judged. As a development it has enriched technique and it is only deplorable when misused.

Tolstoi obviously gave a great deal of consideration to this problem. He often gives what purports to be a transcript of thought, but, when the thinker is in a normal state of mind,

his soliloquy is clearer, more connected, than
would probably have been the case. Dolly,
driving out to the country to visit Anna, falls
into a long reverie which is given, for the most
part, verbatim. It is a more precise piece of
thinking than Dolly's suggested capacities
would warrant. She would not have finished so
many of her sentences. There would have been
all sorts of interruptions and inexplicable allusions. Extreme realism Tolstoi reserves for
those occasions when he wants to depict an
abnormal state of mind—a person distracted.
Anna's thoughts, as she drives to the station
just before her suicide, are no more irrelevant
and inconsequent than those of any woman out
on a morning's shopping. She also, seeing
children running, would think of her son;
reading the name over a bun shop, would in-
stantly remember her youth and how, when
she went riding then, she had red hands. It is
the balance and swing back that are gone.
Every object beheld fans the same flame, feeds
the same despair; even the smell of paint in-
furiates her. Everything perceived is rejected
with disgust. The link between *ego* and *non ego*
is snapping. Had Tolstoi made frequent use of
this kind of realism, when giving us the
thoughts of people like Dolly, he would, so to

speak, have had no shot left in his locker for Anna.

Molly Bloom's long reverie, at the end of *Ulysses*, has often been cited as a triumph of interior monologue. It is indeed; but it, again, is not a transcription of normal thinking. Molly is not in her ordinary, day-time state of mind. She is in that particular trance, familiar to all of us, when we lie awake and images flow past us, half sensuous, half mental, and wholly uncontrolled, because any attempt to focus or direct them would only wake us up and we want to get to sleep. We are not trying to reach any particular conclusion. Yet, in the very order of these ideas, the manner in which they choose to present themselves, there seems to be a kind of significance. We feel dreamily that there might be among them some secret, long known to us and never stated. They have an elusive importance, an importance which is here conveyed by a slow gathering of current and impetus which bears the whole meditation forward to the conclusive mood of the last sentences. It is a superb transcription of the human mind, but only of one infrequent phase of it.

No satisfactory solution has been found. Complete imaginative fusion with the subject,

not often attained by any writer, will sometimes solve the problem for him, and may
carry him far beyond his age, for a moment, in
technical resource. He will do something un-
usual, not done by any of his contemporaries,
and do it instinctively, as though unaware that
it is an innovation. Scott, contented as a rule
with the conventions of his age, breaks with
them sometimes when he is writing of Jeanie
Deans, who, of all his characters, had by far the
strongest hold on him. In giving her thoughts
he indicates those small, subtle changes of style
and vocabulary, dictated by mood, which are
the essence of the whole business; he indicates
them with a certainty for which many a writer
in this century, grinding out interior monologue, might envy him. Jeanie calls her husband Reuben and thinks of him as Reuben.
When she gets that dreadful letter from Effie,
with the fifty pounds, she is particularly taken
aback by Effie's calm injunction that she shall
say nothing of this to Reuben Butler, for fear
that it may get about, and annoy Effie's husband, who is 'as jealous of his family honour
now as ever he was careless about it'. Jeanie's
inward comment is:

'I maun tell the Minister about it. I dinna
see that she suld be sae feared of her ain bonny

bargain o' a gudeman, and that I shouldna reverence Mr. Butler just as much.'

He has become 'the Minister' and 'Mr. Butler' because she is mentally speaking to Effie and speaking rather stiffly.

There are moments in a writer's life when he is so sure of what he has to say that he cannot make a mistake, cannot put a foot wrong. Without conscious effort or deliberation, he does his best work. At such moments he does not need 'technique'. That self-imposed discipline he needs for all the rest of his writing, since write he must, if only for the hope of occasionally writing his best. In the homely struggle with his medium he finds some compensation for the rarity, the unpredictability, of those occasions when he knows himself to be air borne. Nor can he explain to anybody, least of all to himself, why they occur at all, why they occur so seldom, and why he does not always write as well as that.

CHAPTER VI

The Professionals

Towards the end of the nineteenth century, novelists made a determined effort to improve their literary standing. They felt that they had been treated as buskers long enough. They had lived down their disreputable past, they had great achievements to their credit, and it was high time that they were taken seriously. The novel-reading public ought no longer to be reproved for frivolous waste of time.

A kind of amateurishness which had been, perhaps, the chief reproach against the novel must be eliminated. In future merit must be defined upon some recognizable principle. Dogma was needed. Schools of thought were needed. Coteries were needed. All the other artists had had these things for hundreds of years, had had them for so long that they could even afford to rebel against them. Nobody had obliged the novelist with a single fetter which he could throw off.

All this was, at first, more strongly felt in France than in England, where the professional status of the artist has always been unsettled. The novel, in France, had had less traditional popularity. Throughout the eighteenth century it had been an aristocratic amusement. Borrow's old apple woman who spent her days spelling over the history of 'the blessed Mary Flanders', the villagers who assembled on the green every evening to hear the blacksmith read *Pamela*, and who rang a peal on the church bells for her wedding, were peculiarly English. *Manon Lescaut* had less in it for apple women, and nobody could ring church bells for Julie and Saint Preux since they never got to the altar.

The English novel was, moreover, dominated for a long time by such incorrigibles as Hardy and Meredith. Hardy did not scruple to assert that he would have taken a great deal more trouble over *Tess of the D'Urbervilles* had he known that the book was going to be such a success. In a serial version he allowed Angel Clare to push Tess through a stream in a

87

wheelbarrow because the editor feared that
the original passage, in which he carries her in
his arms, might be a little too warm. Meredith
was as bad, if not worse. He wrote the first
chapters of *The Amazing Marriage*, dropped it
for twenty years, and then resumed it without
troubling to read over what he had written.
Carinthia Jane, taken by her husband to a
prize fight immediately after the wedding cere-
mony, is then abandoned by him on the door-
step of an inn. The subsequent birth of their
child gives the reader a great start. It would
appear to be a case of parthenogenesis. A few
scattered paragraphs near the end of the book
hint at an explanation. These were inserted by
Meredith when he discovered that he had forgotten to write an important chapter. To call
such methods professional was more than anyone felt able to do.

It is not surprising that the three leading
English professionals were an American, an
Irishman, and a Pole. Henry James was the
most explicit concerning his own technique.
George Moore was the most doctrinaire. Conrad
had the most illuminating things to say about
other people. His comments on Maupassant
would have been an excellent guide to that
writer, could the young Maupassant have read

them at the beginning of his career. All three were tremendously interested in the theory of the novel; they believed that a writer ought to be able to determine in advance what a good novel should be, instead of writing one, as their forbears had done, in the hope that it would turn out to be good. Arnold Bennett thought so too, but he could never manage to be a strict professional. He was too romantic a gallophile and more determined to write as like a Frenchman as possible than to write according to cocker.

The notion of a professional recipe did make some headway. Schools of thought did, to some extent, grow up. Novelists, in the first decade of this century, wore a very respectable air. They took to living in coteries round Rye and Winchelsea, and they had *The English Review* as a vehicle for their ideas. Their position, as men of letters, was never quite what it would have been in Paris, but it was greatly improved, especially if they also wrote poetry. Even the incorrigibles profited. The novel was in some degree liberated from its servitude to popular favour. There were to be no more apple women, no more church bells, no more Wizards of the North, no more stampedes for the latest instalment of Dick Swiveller. *Punch*

G   89

began to be respectful to people who had, in the past, been glad enough to get a patronizing slap on the back from Baron de Bookeworm. When Meredith died he merited a full-page cartoon with the handsomest trappings in the way of laurel wreaths. By 1928, when Hardy achieved an Abbey funeral, novelists were talking glibly and publicly of their integrity.

This doughty watchword was very much in the air at the time, and had come up during the hullabaloo over the French Impressionist painters. Nobody had thought very much about it until people who disliked the Impressionists accused them of dishonesty, declaring that they painted with their tongues in their cheeks in order to create a sensation. The defenders of these painters loudly and justly declared that they were men of the highest integrity. After a while everybody began to like the Impressionists. Since integrity had been the word most often used in connexion with them, a notion got about that they were good painters because they had it, and that it is, in itself, a guarantee of merit. The fact that bad artists can have it too was not so generally recognized.

To the novelists it was like a crest and a coat of arms to a parvenu. It was displayed with ostentation as a proof that they were as well born as everybody else on Parnassus. To be sure they had integrity! They had quite as much of it as Manet and Monet.

The word was anxiously applied to the great dead, since an academic criticism had emerged which largely occupied itself with purity of intentions. Had they had enough of it? Not all of them, unfortunately. Thackeray was discovered to have displayed a 'cynical attitude' over his work. He went down to the bottom of the class. Dickens was not cynical, and went up. Scott's integrity was 'worse than nothing, for it was a purely moral and commercial integrity'. He was stood in the corner. As for Kipling, he was sent to Borstal.

A great effort was made to distinguish the novel written out of creative impulse from the potboiler. This was not easy, since a first rate potboiler is likely to be better written, to be far more worth the money and attention of the reader, than a tenth-rate work of art. But there is a point of distinction, whereby the one may be disentangled from the other, whatever their respective merits. Lamb, in a letter to Wordsworth, written in 1801, put it thus:

'It appears to me a fault in *The Beggar*, that the instructions conveyed in it are too direct and like a lecture; they don't slide into the mind of the reader when he is imagining no such thing. An intelligent reader finds a sort of insult in being told: I will teach you how to think upon this subject. This fault, if I am right, is in a ten thousandth degree worse in many many novelists and modern poets who continually put up a sign-post to show where you are to feel. They set out with assuming their readers to be stupid. Very different from *Robinson Crusoe* . . . and other beautiful bare narratives. There is implied an unwritten compact between author and reader: I will tell you a story and I suppose you will understand it. Modern novels, *St. Leons* and the like, are full of such flowers as these: Let not my reader suppose! . . . Imagine, if you can! Modest!'

Jane Austen was saying the same thing, in effect, when she parodied Marmion:

I do not write for such dull elves
As have not a great deal of ingenuity themselves.

It is improbable that any two writers would ever quite agree in their definition of that imaginary reader from whom they want their intended response. It is held by some that they are simply addressing themselves. Others admit to addressing a composite being, possessed of more faculties of response than are ever likely to be united in a single mind. Others address somebody never met, never to be met, but existing, so they confidently believe, somewhere in cosmos. To some a single mind represents the summit of human understanding, as Burke's mind was to Crabbe.

Yet there is one point upon which all would agree. Whatever attributes they devise for this faceless, nameless being, they never suppose him to be stupid. They cannot think of him as, in any way, inferior to themselves. On the contrary, they invest him with perceptions, imagination, and intellect superior to their own. He has the best mind of which they are able to conceive. No artist, when at work, is troubled by the knowledge that he will doubtless be read by very stupid people. With the compulsion to write comes the instinctive assurance that he will be understood, if only he can present what he has to say in a manner worthy of that best mind. Should he fail, the fault will lie with him, not with the other. It will be his own stupidity which will intercept the message. If he takes great pains to make himself clear it is not because he is afraid that fools will miss the point, but because intelligence demands clarity. The objections which haunt him are not the cavillings of the slow-witted but the comments of the quick-witted. And he will, moreover, write with the intention of being re-read, although he knows very well that it is wasted labour. He will be in luck if anybody reads what he has written once, with anything like close attention. Yet this reasonable certainty does not prevent him from catering for the first impression and for the renewed impression, since the whole of what he has to say comprises both. That is how a genuine novelist works.

The stature of that best conceivable mind must vary with the stature of the writer. Should he possess but slender powers in the way of intellect and imagination, his ideal mind might strike some people as being pretty commonplace. His Burke is no giant, but is still the best that he can devise. For this reason there is a good deal of confused thinking about the validity, in intention, of inferior art, since it appears to be addressed to the stupid, although it is produced in perfectly good faith. Should it meet with popular success it is thought to be potboiling. This accusation is often undeserved. The only crime committed by a bad artist is to have produced bad art, but he does not do this on purpose. Many a crude novelette, beneath critical attention, has, nevertheless, been written in strict observance of Lamb's implied compact. Breaches of that compact, little sign-posts, deliberate nudges to the stupid, can, on the other hand, be detected sometimes in very stately pages.

A distinction between art and non-art may be useful, but it is not the most vital distinction to be made. The major service of criticism is to distinguish between bad art and good art, and, above all, to help us to understand why good art is good. It was a great misfortune for the cause of the novel that criticism should have gone off on a witch-hunting excursion, just when novelists had a chance of securing serious attention. They were not the only sufferers. Some attempt was also made, in the 1930's, to screen the poets for suspicious intentions and cynical attitudes, but the poets are better established. Enough sense has been talked about them, in the course of 2,500 years, to enable them to stand up against an occasional bombardment of nonsense. The case of the novelists was not so robust. Their public, long accustomed to think of them with a certain degree of disparagement, would have been reluctant enough, in any case, to change its ideas. An opportunity was missed of establishing an art, claimed as great, by defining those qualities which make it so. It was neglected in favour of denunciations against naughty boys.

Criticism based upon a scrutiny of intentions may be effective in distinguishing between art and non-art, since it should be adroit in detecting those signposts, however pretentiously they may be disguised. It is less well equipped for the task of distinguishing between bad art and good art since both, whatever gulf lies between them, are ruled by the same intentions. As far as we know, Mrs. Henry Wood was as much in earnest as George Eliot. It is not by a yard-stick of intentions that we can measure the distance between *East Lynne* and *Middlemarch*.

CHAPTER VII

Dogma

Dogma was needed and dogma was forth-coming. With the growth of the professional movement emerged the disposition to believe that some one particular way of writing a novel must be the only possible and permissible way. For this reason a certain technical approach, known in France as naturalism, in England as realism, acquired for a while a categorical im-portance. It became a test of merit. Unrealistic writers were, *ipso facto*, bad writers.

It acquired this importance because, just at the time when dogma was urgently sought, it happened to be engaging the attention of many good writers. It offered them a new range of subjects and new treatment; it enabled them to say some things which had not been said before.

It had, besides, certain attributes much prized in the epoch. The conventional were liable to be shocked by it, since it entailed plain statement upon some topics hitherto banned to the novelist. To shock somebody, in 1900, was desirable; all the other artists had been very turbulent, had been causing riots, for a hundred years. A riot or two over the novel might improve its status.

In the early realistic novel Flora's validity was established by surrounding her with intensely valid detail, of a kind which the reader could readily endorse from his own experience. If she cooked cabbage the house smelt of it. If the weather was warm she sweated. If she went to Penzance she started from Paddington and took a train which could be verified in Bradshaw. If she died she did so of an authentic disease described in clinical detail. Any doctor, reading an account of her symptoms, would agree that she had to die. No author could save her after 'a coffee grounds vomit'.

This detail need not necessarily be sordid or disgusting; it was a matter of plain accuracy. The whole technique however came to be identified with the unseemly statement, because it was this aspect of it which most struck the average reader. He had never met such things

in a novel before; a 'realistic novel' not only
mentioned a privy but described minutely what
went on there. Many realistic novels used such
material sparingly, but liberty to employ clo-
acal, physical, or sexual detail was interpreted,
by so many inferior novelists, as licence that
the whole nature of the technique came to be
misunderstood.

In the hands of a master this use of detail,
with its appeal to universal experience, can
drive home the truth of imagined experience.
Vronsky's toothache, an agony with which
most readers are acquainted, is employed to
convince us of an agony which few have
plumbed—the sensations of a man whose mistress has thrown herself under a train. On his
last appearance in the book he is nearly mad
with toothache, his jaw twitching, his face so
twisted that he can hardly speak naturally. He
can think of nothing else. A short conversation
with a friend whom he has not met since his
disaster, the sight of a railway tender smoothly
rolling along the line, deliver him to 'a different
pain, not an ache, but an inner trouble, that
set his whole being in anguish'. For an instant
he forgets his toothache and remembers a scene
to which we have had, so far, only oblique refer-
ences, but which cannot be allowed to happen

quite off stage. We know now what he saw when he rushed into the cloak-room of another railway station and beheld what was left of Anna.

In lesser hands the effect on the reader might have been to suggest that Vronsky was not really heart-broken, since the memory of Anna had been so easily effaced by toothache. In lesser hands there would probably have been too much toothache already in the book. Unimportant people would have had it at irrelevant moments.

Balzac was another expert at using significant detail at the right moment, and so was Arnold Bennett. Elsie, the maid in *Riceyman Steps*, keeps her umbrella under her bed. An ardent but uncritical admirer of Bennett asked how he could possibly have known this. It was just where Elsie would keep her umbrella, but how did he find it out? To this reader, to any reader responding to an expert piece of realism, the effect was one of Elsie acting and Bennett relating her doings. She was a creature living in his attics, into whose bedroom he had taken a surreptitious peep, rather than his creation and obliged to keep her umbrella wherever he might choose.

For a while it was maintained that a good novel must be full of toothache and umbrellas.

Writers who neglected them got lowe₁ marks than writers who used them badly. At length it became clear that there is no intrinsic magic in the formula, since it can do little for a writer who has no Vronsky and no Elsie. The imagined material is still the essence of the business; a formula can beget nothing on the imagination. The entire dogma became discredited by those who abused it. A critic in the 1920's used to give an amusing description of his premature relief after reading a novel which he described as a sojourn in *Cloaca Maxima*. 'At last!' he thought, 'somebody has said it all,—everything! So now, perhaps, they will have to stop, since they can only go on saying the same thing.' Unfortunately they were perfectly prepared to do this. *Tout est dit* is a knell which rings in the ears of good artists only. Realism, however, as dogma, began to go out, although plenty of writers still use it because it suits them.

Dogma seldom makes a dramatic exit. Too many people have put their shirts on it and, although they may have lost faith, they have testified too long and too loudly to be anxious to eat their words. They prefer to declare that these words have perhaps a slightly different and more general meaning. Realism today does not mean what it meant fifty years ago. It is no longer an affair of saucepans and railway time-tables, but is generally applied to likelihood in human behaviour. It is a word which comes up in any argument as to the warrant which normal human experience might give to the conduct of characters in a novel. By normal human experience, most debaters mean their own, and the argument generally founders on a reef of opposing standards. I know nobody who would behave like that! I know plenty of people who would behave like that! What prigs your friends must be! What scum *your* friends must be!

A novel is most likely to be called 'unrealistic' if the behaviour of the characters is something superior. Few of us mind admitting that there may be worse swine in the world than any whom we have yet had the misfortune to meet. A book in which the characters, when shipwrecked, eat each other, is allowed to be realistic, although we may not be personally acquainted with cannibals. It is not so pleasant to allow that standards of conduct higher than those prevailing down our street are probable, prevalent, or convincing. Nettled, as was the woman in the Welsh village who learnt that a neighbour's daughter was about to be married, although not pregnant, we are inclined to exclaim: There's snob for you!

Mr. O'Connor uses the word in its contemporary sense when he complains that Jane Austen's heroines, for all their feminine qualities, are none of them liars, which is, he says, 'magnificent but not realism'. It was not used in this sense fifty years ago, or even thirty years ago, when Desmond MacCarthy found Proust unrealistic on the score of 'glaring improbabilities which are recounted with careful circumstantial detail'. * Here the suggestion was that Proust did not always make sure that Swann caught the right express for Lyons. Realism and unrealism today mean little more than agreement or disagreement with the writer's point of view. They have no bearing on technical form.

An alternative dogma was taking shape when Mr. Forster gave the Clark lectures. For some time writers had been rebelling against this dreary search under the bed for more convincing detail. Virginia Woolf gave voice to that revolt in 1919, in an essay on fiction, later published in *The Common Reader*. Here she

* *Criticism*, Desmond MacCarthy.

speaks up for the novel of egocentric perception. She does not claim that it ought to be the only permissible novel; that claim was made later, by others, when the dogma had crystallized. She merely says: 'Any method is right, every method is right, that expresses what we wish to express, if we are writers; that brings us closer to the novelist's intention if we are readers.' She states the case for her own method and that against the realists, whom she calls the materialists.

'They write of unimportant things . . . they spend immense skill and immense industry making the trivial and the transitory appear the true and the enduring.'

As might be expected, she trains her heaviest guns upon Arnold Bennett, since he, of all the English realists, is the most difficult to dislodge. He is the 'worst culprit'. Of Galsworthy she merely complains that she does not find what she seeks in his pages. In Bennett's pages no seeker, of any description, is likely to discover anything at all.

'His characters live abundantly, even unexpectedly, but it remains to ask how do they live, and what do they live for? . . . Is it worth while? What is the point of it all? Can it be that, owing to one of those little deviations which the human spirit seems to make from time to time, Mr. Bennett has come down with his magnificent apparatus for catching life just an inch or two on the wrong side? Life escapes; and perhaps without life nothing else is worth while. . . . Whether we call it life or spirit, truth or reality, this, the essential thing, has moved off, or on. . . . So much of the enormous labour of proving the solidity, the likeness to life, of the story is not merely labour thrown away but labour misplaced to the extent of obscuring and blotting out the light of the conception. The writer seems constrained . . . to provide a plot, to provide comedy, tragedy, love interest, and an air of probability embalming the whole so impeccable that if all his figures were to come to life they would find themselves dressed down to the last button of their coats in the fashion of the hour. . . . Is life like this? Must novels be like this?

'Look within and life, it seems, is very far from being "like this". Examine for a moment an ordinary mind on an ordinary day. The mind receives a myriad impressions—trivial, fantastic, evanescent, or engraved with the sharpness of steel. From all sides they come, an incessant shower of innumerable atoms; and as they fall, as they shape themselves into the life of Monday or Tuesday, the accent falls differently from of old; the moment of importance came not here but there; so that, if a writer were a free man and not a slave, if he could write what he chose, not what he must, if he could base his work upon his own feeling and not upon convention, there would be no plot, no comedy, no tragedy, no love interest or catastrophe in the accepted style, and perhaps not a single button sewn on as Bond Street tailors would have it. Life is not a series of gig lamps symmetrically arranged; life is a luminous halo, a semi-transparent envelope surrounding us from the beginning of consciousness to the end. Is it not the task of the novelist to convey this varying, this unknown and uncircumscribed spirit, whatever aberration or complexity it may display, with as little mixture of the alien and the external as possible?'

This is a round statement of what might be called the Proustian stance, an attitude which may be observed in many writers who have little else in common with Proust. It looks within. It bases all on the writer's own feeling. It shuns the external. On that ticklish question of validity it would say: The cat I see: the cat I

106

remember: the cat I imagine: Is there a pin of difference between these three cats? They are all images in my mind; that they are there is the only warrant I can offer for the existence of any of them. You accuse me of inventing Flora? You might as well accuse me of inventing the Queen. In a way I have done so. My idea of the Queen is not exactly anybody else's idea of her. I offer you nothing that is not in my mind, my memory, my imagination. I know no other source of truth, and I do not drag in external objects, umbrellas and so forth, as witnesses to what I say.

Proust himself had singular advantages in adopting this stance, since he was a Frenchman and a Parisian. The chief objection to the egocentric novel is its limited orbit. The author, browsing only on the pasture of his personal perceptions, deliberately oblivious of all beyond them, can easily convey a sense of restriction. He writes from an ivory tower, withdrawn and secluded, inhabited apparently by a little coterie of people who never read the newspaper and could not mend a blown fuse. Of Proust, Desmond MacCarthy says, that he 'does not check his own impressions by the common stock of experience which mankind has accumulated'. No egocentric does this; such experience is external and alien. But a Parisian's certainty that Paris is cosmos can often, for a while, win us into acquiescence; we almost believe that nothing beyond his perception counts for much. It was a typical, if legendary, Parisian who went up the Eiffel Tower every day because the doctor had ordered mountain air.

No English writer can enjoy this magnificent arrogance. Beyond the range of his own perception he is, whether he likes it or not, aware of other places, other people. They impinge upon his private vision and ruffle it. On the frontiers of his grazing ground there are these alien yahoos, these tough men with the lie in the soul; they engage in trades and professions; they tell limericks in tap-rooms; they read the newspaper and mend fuses; they are a deadly menace to the sensitive grazer, and their female companions are, if anything, more dangerous. The egocentric novel is easier for a Frenchman than an Englishman.

It is perhaps easier for a woman than a man. Seclusion suits a woman better. It suited Emily Brontë, who made a solitary excursion into this field, more than a hundred years ago. As a woman she was able to display a grand obliviousness to practical detail which her admirers might find a little more daunting in a

man. Heathcliff, a penniless and unlettered
hind, vanishes from the story for three years.
He returns a man of substance. In this very
short interval he has not only made a fortune
but has also, to judge by his command of
language, found the time to put himself
through a university course. How did he manage to do all this? His creator would have said
that it is unimportant. Such details are among
the trivial and transitory things over which
realists waste their skill and industry. They
have no more significance than the shape of
Heathcliff's toothbrush, if he used one. Readers
who want information on such points are not
likely to care for anything that Emily Brontë
has to say. This lofty disregard of the affairs of
the market-place comes more naturally from a
woman than from a man. Nobody expects her
to read the newspaper; she can do so if she
likes, but she is not thought singular if she prefers to light the fire with it. A man who does
not read it is liable to be slightly on the defensive.

To the egocentric novelist a railway time
table is not Holy Writ. We may not catch him
sending Flora to Penzance from Liverpool
Street. He may take trouble over accuracy, as
he takes trouble over correcting misprints in

his proofs; he regards it as a chore; for him, it has nothing to do with validity.

This method was sponsored by some very influential people in the literary world, including those who formed what came to be known as the Bloomsbury Group. It was not, by them, recommended to the rank and file as dogma, since the rank and file was not expected to be up to it; by its first advocates it was regarded as a formula for the rare, the gifted, the chosen few. The subsequent vogue for the 'novel of sensibility', as it was sometimes called, was none of their doing; they had no great taste for vogues of any kind. But so many notable Mandarins came down in praise of it that there was no holding the lesser Mandarins, and sensibility, for a while, was all the reading. Amongst novelists the good news spread that they need no longer provide plot, comedy, tragedy, love interest nor catastrophe in order to get top marks. Many adopted the new method who had never got nearer to Bloomsbury than Clapham Junction. They did not see why they should not be as rare and gifted and chosen as anybody else. Among those who did not take it over lock, stock, and barrel, few were so strong minded as to refrain from a few bravura passages, indicating the luminous halo, just to show what they could do in that line if they liked.

The particular skill involved lies in selection and in the juxtaposition of the images offered. The same might be said of any narrative form, but others allow, will not suffer from, a more rough and ready treatment. This one takes the novel closest to the frontiers of poetry. Things perceived, things remembered, things imagined, are all woven into a single tapestry, all invested with the same quality. The object is, as always, to present the imagined thing. The method is to refine away, as far as possible, the difference in essence between the three strands in the fabric.

The necessary gift, if the imagined thing is to be presented thus, lies in a perceptive sensibility to all that is not imagined. To all must be imparted the same unique flavour. Homer might invariably describe the sea as wine dark, or fishy, because he spoke of everybody's sea. The egocentric may never use a conventional epithet. He must, if he mentions the sea, make it *his* sea, as perceived by him alone. Should he possess the necessary gifts he does this naturally. It is his sea. He does not have to rack his brains for something very striking and original to say about the sea. It is only when the gifts are

111

lacking that a strained effect is produced, and the reader grows restive. He rebels against an author who is continually making clever remarks, and who cannot mention nightfall without saying that the crows, stringing out across the sunset sky, looked like old ladies coming out of church. He thinks, with some nostalgia, of those Victorian authors who would have been content to state that it was evening when our hero set out on his errand. The fact that this novel has no hero and no errand, merely a plethora of sensitive remarks about the crows, puts him out of patience with sensibility.

Affectations of this kind, in writers who should never have attempted the method, together with the exaggerated claims made on its behalf, engendered considerable hostility among writers and critics who thought that there were other ways of writing a novel. This hostility fed an antagonism already awakened by a certain inflection of arrogance in the utterances of some of the Bloomsbury Group. Prejudice forthwith ascribed arrogance to all of them, although there had been none in Virginia Woolf's defence of the egocentric novel. This reputation restricted the influence of some very valuable ideas, and of an uncompromising emphasis upon the first rate. Cultural standards, associated with a group, are always in this kind of danger. The first rate cannot have too many champions, but it is least well served by those who allow it to be suspected that they regard their own value for it as a personal asset.

As soon as a number of inexcusably bad novels of sensibility had been written, the opposition opened fire. The dogma collapsed so suddenly that those who had put their shirts on it had no resource save to declare furiously that the whole art of the novel must be, in such a case, defunct.

That it is, and always will be, a method for the few is probably true. Yet it would be a great disaster if those few did not continue to explore the frontier land between the novel and poetry. This is a territory won to literature by those professionals who broke up the enormous novel-reading public, the public accumulated by the Victorians, into smaller and more manageable groups. The tastes of readers have become more specialized. There is now a large public for such writers as Elizabeth Bowen and Eudora Welty, who would not, fifty years ago, have had a platform from which to speak.

Crabbe, born too soon, was lost to an art which might have claimed him in this century. He took refuge on the wrong side of the fence, although he was, in essence, a novelist. His tapestry, woven from perception, memory and imagination, suffers from the jog trot of uninspired couplets, from the constriction of a form unsuited to it. A little less than poetry, it is never, in its finest passages, less than poetic. In prose it would have been more so. He has long been the novelists' poet because he said things which his true comrades, on the other side of the fence, would have given their eyes to say. They do not thus envy the achievements of born poets. Nor does he, in born poets, awaken that start of recognition, that inward exclamation: *Ah! He was one of us!* The stature of a lost novelist can be perceived in the dream of the condemned highwayman, roused suddenly on the morning of his execution by the shout of a watchman outside the prison. Memory and imagination are exquisitely blended. The young Crabbe, wandering by a sleepy sea, is one with the wretched soul, snatched from safety.

Yes, all are with him now, and all the while
Life's early prospects, with his Fanny, smile.
Then come his sister and his village friend,
And he will now the sweetest moments spend
Life has to yield;—No! Never will he find
Again on earth such pleasure to his mind.

Dogma

He goes through shrubby walks these friends
   among:
Love in their looks and honour on the tongue.
Nay,there'sacharmbeyondwhatnatureshows,
The bloom is softer and more sweetly glows.
They feel the calm delight, and thus proceed
Through the green lane,—then linger on the
   mead. . . .
Then cross the bounding brook they make their
   way
O'er its rough bridge,—and there behold the
   bay!
The ocean smiling to the fervid sun—
The waves that softly fall and slowly run—
The ships at distance and the boats at hand:
And now they walk upon the sea side sand,
Counting the number and what kind they be,—
Ships softly sinking in the sleepy sea.
Now arm in arm, now parted, they behold
The glittering water on the shingles rolled:
The timid girls, half dreading their design,
Dip the small foot in the retarded brine. . . .
Pearl shells and rubied star fish they admire,
And will arrange above the parlour fire,
Tokens of bliss—Oh! Horrible! A wave
Roars as it rises. 'Save me, Edward, save!'
She cries.—Alas! The watchman on his way
Calls and lets in—truth, terror, and the day.

CHAPTER VIII

The Choice

A woman goes into a room full of people and
makes an immediate impression upon them by
her beauty. This event has been described by a
great many novelists in a great many ways, of
which some examples are here offered. In no
case is the effect upon any particular beholder
of importance. That would widen the field too
much. It is the effect upon the group, and her
attitude, which is presented.

(1) AUTOBIOGRAPHICAL

The full triumph of complete success, to
which everything else is subordinate, is particularly well conveyed in this form. The other
characters can be reduced to a single dimension;
they exist merely to pay tribute.

'This alcove fronts the longest gravel-walk in the garden, so that they saw me most of the way I came; and my master told me afterwards, with pleasure, all they said of me. . . . They all, I saw, which abashed me, stood at the windows, and in the doorway, looking full at me. . . . Lady Jones said: "She is a charming creature, I can see that at this distance." And Sir Simon, it seems, who has been a sad rake in his younger days, swore he never saw so easy an air, so fine a shape, and so graceful a presence. The Lady Darnford said, I was a sweet girl. And Mrs. Peters said very handsome things. Even the parson said I should be the pride of the county. . . . The young ladies blushed and envied me.

'When I came near, he saw me in a little confusion, and was so kind as to meet me. "Give me your hand," said he, "my good girl; you walk too fast." I did so, with a curtsy; and he leading me up the steps of the alcove, in a most gentlemanlike manner, presented me to the ladies, who all saluted me, and said they hoped to be better acquainted with me; and Lady Darnford was pleased to say, I should be the flower of their neighbourhood. Sir Simon said, "Good neighbour, by your leave," and saluting me, added, "Now I will say, that I have kissed the loveliest maiden in England." . . . Mr. Peters very gravely followed his example, and said, like a bishop, "God bless you, fair excellence." '

This triumph over Mr. Peters, the parson, is the apex of success, for he took a very different line, only a few weeks earlier. The good young curate appealed to him to rescue this fair excellence from abduction, imprisonment, maltreatment, and probable rape. He then said:

'What, and embroil myself with a man of Mr. B's power and fortune? No, not I, I'll assure you. . . . Her shyness will procure her good terms enough . . . and 'tis what all young gentlemen will do.'

Now that this hypocrite has been forced to change his tune his tribute is as complacently received as though it came from an unimpeachable source. To recall his former conduct would be to allow that his commendation was not really worth much. That would take off from the triumph. The intoxication of success, the tricks which it can play with any real sense of values, is best conveyed by the person who feels it. The narrator, describing it on her behalf, would find it more difficult not to remind us of what is now obliterated. To say: 'Mr. Peters called her fair excellence, and kissed her, whereupon she felt that he was a very good man and enjoyed all the pleasure of a good man's praise,' would be to tell this story rather differently.

(2) THE AUTHOR-OBSERVER

A description of our beauty's appearance is a task most safely accomplished by the Author-Observer. The impersonal narrator cannot embark so fearlessly upon a catalogue of nose, eyes, curls, and dimples, for the reader might protest that all this leaves him cold. The Author-Observer can boldly exalt his own taste in beauty, since he is there in person, and the reader is at liberty to disagree with him. It is, after all, not his task to convince the reader that she was beautiful, but merely that the people in the room found her so.

'Fanny sat likewise down by the fire. . . . She presently engaged the eyes of the host, his wife, the maid of the house, and the young fellow who was their guide; they all conceived that they had never seen anything half so handsome; and indeed, reader, if thou art of an amorous hue, I advise thee to skip over the next paragraph, which, to render our history perfect, we are obliged to set down, humbly hoping that we may escape the fate of

119

Pygmalion. . . . Fanny was now in the nineteenth year of her age; she was tall and delicately shaped; but not one of those slender young women who seem rather intended to hang up in the hall of an anatomist than for any other purpose. On the contrary, she was so plump that she seemed bursting through her tight stays, especially in the part which confined her swelling breasts. Nor did her hips want the assistance of a hoop to extend them . . . her eyes black and sparkling; her nose just inclining to the Roman; her lips red and moist, etc., etc.'

This description may not inflame the reader quite as much as Fanny's creator feared that it might. It is completely unromantic, but it leaves us in no doubt as to what it was at which the company stared. The fact that Fanny bursting through her stays might not have been thought so handsome at any other period does not prevent the reader from accepting the scene; a change in taste does not affect its validity. The impersonal narrator could not have risked such a description since he might have been supposed to set up a universal and timeless standard of beauty. The Author-Observer, with his frank enthusiasm, is merely among those present.

120

(3) IMPERSONAL NARRATIVE

This lady is simply described as looking like a goddess. The reader can interpret this as he pleases. That is how she strikes two young men who are visiting her husband and have heard a great deal about her, although they never met her before. Her beauty and her past are fabulous; in an earlier story, to which this is the sequel, she had only to enter a room for everyone present to fall silent. This has given a great deal of trouble, to her and to everyone else. She has now found a protective way of coming into a room; it is calculated to diminish the impact on the beholders. She comes in with a bevy of maids who set up a housewifely bustle.

'Adreste drew up for her a comfortable chair, Alcippe brought a rug of the softest wool, while Phylo carried her silver work basket . . . a basket that ran on castors and was made of silver finished with a rim of gold. . . . It was full of fine spun yarn, and the spindle with its deep blue wool was laid across it. Helen sat down on the chair, which had a stool below it for her feet, and proceeded at once to find out from her husband what was going on.'

The narrative of this writer is always factual. He makes no comment. His epithets and adjectives are conventional. He enters into no long examination of thoughts, although he sometimes lets us know when his characters think one thing and say another. Nor does he examine their feelings. They rejoice, they laugh, they are wroth, they weep; he indicates to what degree of intensity. He simply states what they say and do. No author was ever less among those present. It is the reader who is expected to be present and to draw his own conclusions from this parade of rugs and footstools and work baskets. We are not told that the young men found it easier to refrain from staring than they had expected, and were able to continue a decorous conversation with their host. Why should we be told so, if we have the wit to guess? Why should the amusement of those who guess be spoilt by a signpost for donkeys?

(4) THE REALIST

The dress in which this fourth woman makes her entrance has been described a few pages earlier:

'It was of pale blue taffetas striped in a darker blue, with the corsage cut in basques, and the underskirt of a similar taffeta, but unstriped. The effect of the ornate overskirt falling on the plain underskirt with its small double *volant* was, she thought, . . . adorable. The waist was higher than any she had had before, and the crinoline expansive. Tied round her head with a large bow and flying blue ribbons under the chin, was a fragile flat *capote* like a baby's bonnet, which allowed her hair to escape in front and her great chignon behind. A large spotted veil flew out from the *capote* over the chignon. . . . This day, because it was the first day of her French frock, she regarded as her *début* in the dizzy life of capitals. She existed in a rapture of bliss, an ecstasy which could feel no fatigue, either of body or spirit.'

This writer could probably have given as exact a description of any dress worn by the lady. Since he knew his craft he kept detail for an important dress and an important occasion. He dwells on these technicalities because the dress must be, in its way, as real as she is. It has a part of its own to play in the minds of others.

'As the *chasseur* held open the door for them to enter, and Sophia passed modestly into the glowing yellow interior of the restaurant, followed by Gerald in his character of man-of-the-world, they drew the attention of Sylvain's numerous and glittering guests. No face could have made a more provocative contrast to the women's faces in those screened rooms than the face of Sophia, so childlike between the baby's bonnet and the huge bow of ribbon, so candid, so charmingly conscious of its own pure beauty and of the fact that she was no longer a virgin, but the equal in knowledge of any woman alive. She saw around her, clustered about the white tables, multitudes of violently red lips, powdered cheeks, cold, hard eyes, self-possessed arrogant faces, and insolent bosoms. . . . They frightened her: they appeared to her so corrupt and so proud in their corruption. . . . As for them, they marvelled at the phenomena presented in Sophia's person; they admired; they admitted the style of the gown; but they envied neither her innocence nor her beauty; they envied nothing but her youth and the fresh tint of her cheeks.

' "Encore des Anglais!" said some of them, as if that explained all.'

The visual validity of all this is used to spotlight Sophia at a particular crisis in her story. If she were not focused at the centre of the scene it would merely be a piece of distinguished reporting. She is an aria with full orchestral accompaniment. But the Restaurant would get on very well without her, playing

124

some other tune, and she, without damage, could be extricated from this scene and placed in some other.

(5) THE EGOCENTRIC

The fifth girl and her setting are one. Each contributes to the existence of the other. Both are pinpointed in time. At no other moment, before or after, would she, the room, or the company, be exactly like this. A second minute further towards nightfall and the scene has melted into something else; she has taken a step forward in time.

'Jane entered a drawing-room black and white at the door end with standing men. As she advanced towards them the sound track stopped. Bowers of flowers cascaded fern mist from the piano top; jaded late green heat came in at the open windows. The room, more quenched, less dazzling than that above by being a minute further towards nightfall, was overcast by the outdoor rise of lawns and encased in walls of transparent blue. Brought to a standstill under all these eyes by the slight shock of the sense of her own beauty, Jane said, "Lady Latterly will be late," for the first time wondering why. A woman, the apparently only other, diagonal in a black dress on a white sofa,

125

nodded tardily at her over a picture paper, then took a cigarette out of a box—scoffingly, she had lighted it for herself before the group had so far collected its wits as to break ranks. Who knew where they had all come from? The girl, at the advantage of being less surprised by them than they were by her, detachedly heard the silence break up into a clash of experimental, isolated remarks.'

In this writer's work every line is so closely knit into a general design that a quoted extract suffers some slight mutilation. This description is intended, as is every other description, to give a sense of passing time. Each is a stage in a process of emotional preparation; one moment melting into another leads up to the *event,*—which occurs in the last sentence of the book.

Failure to understand the purpose and uses of the method selected, failure to recognize its limitations or to comply with its discipline—such a failure ultimately damns a novelist. Yet in every period there have been many who simply selected the form in vogue at the moment, without ever asking themselves why it should be used, without attempting to understand its requirements. Some very good writers have, of course, made a few mistakes whilst experimenting and feeling their way towards their own technique. Jane Austen began by following in the footsteps of Richardson and Burney; she attempted a novel in letters. She soon saw that this form would never do for her, and abandoned it. No genuine novelist has ever continued in such an error for long.

To examine the rubbish carts of former periods is not easy; their contents are seldom preserved. But when curiosity leads us to explore the attic bookshelves of some old country house, so large that nothing there has ever been thrown away, books come to light which astonish us by their fantastic incompetence. They bear the imprint of respectable publishers. They were, apparently, once reviewed and read. They are now so unreadable that it is not even possible to laugh at them.

It is not that they seem dated, or that they observe conventions which also bound the major writers of their period. It is not that they exhibit some technical clumsiness very common at that time. The incredible thing is that they should ever have been mistaken for novels.

An attempt to study them, to make out what

the author thought he was doing, is tedious but instructive. It will often appear that the content might not have been unpromising and that he had characters which could have taken on some semblance of life, had he ever for a moment considered the form in which they were to be presented. He seems to have shut his eyes and fished his form out of a hat. Here we find a Miss Mattie obliged to tell her own story; a Tommy Traddles entrusted with the history of a David Copperfield; an Author-Observer who introduces no characters, sets no scene, and merely ambles into view quite late in the book in order to hold up the action while he harangues the reader. Here we find the corset covers and armpits of misapplied realism. Here sometimes, in a slightly less faded cover, we find an unfiltered 'stream of consciousness'—an early and clumsy attempt at the egocentric form.

All these writers took it for granted that a novel had to be autobiographical, had to rely on a fictitious narrator, had to contain a few chats with the reader, had, in fact, to be written in a particular way. The reading public apparently shares these illusions. If a novel bears a strong resemblance to all the other novels coming out at the moment, it will swallow the

thing with the vast resignation of the literate.
The vogue, while it lasts, will mask the stupidity of these writers. When it changes, they
founder.

We wonder at the fantastic tastelessness of
our forbears. Then, as we descend the attic
stairs, we begin to speculate about those books
still lodged below in more honourable quarters.
Which of them will eventually find their way
to limbo? Regretfully we dismiss the temptation
to pass sentence on Messrs. X, Y, and Z, because we do not care for what they say, although they know how to write. About content
there can be no prophecy. We perceive that we
should do better to inquire into our own bad
taste. What of those books which we allow to be
readable, even if we do not think them remarkable? Somebody will some day raise their
eyebrows at us and to the attic will go a fresh
batch of throw-outs. It might be safe to pro-
phesy that some of these will be rich in
sensitive remarks about the crows.

During the thirties, when the egocentric
novel was enjoying its boom, it was pretty easy
for a writer without the necessary gifts, without
suitable material, without any real comprehen-
sion of the method, to select this form and
escape whipping. For him, and for his readers,

crows looking like old ladies were the thing, and these crows therefore were liable to crop up in contexts where they had no business to be.

Much is permissible to a writer working in one method, which is absolutely forbidden to those using another. Not that any writer cannot learn a great deal from studying a technique other than his own. George Moore insisted that no artist can sincerely admire work which is the opposite of his own, but Moore was a confirmed dogmatist. A respectful study of some method, which a writer himself never intends to adopt, may reveal a great deal to him. It is especially likely to show him his own shortcomings in the matter of carelessness; every method fosters some of these. It also enlarges his understanding of the infinite variety of things which there are to be said, even though it may confirm his belief that he had better, himself, be silent about a good many of them.

The fifth example given at the beginning of this chapter is taken from Elizabeth Bowen's *A World of Love*. There are passages in this book which her colleagues may admire extremely yet never wish to have written themselves, since in their own work it would never do. There is an account of Big Ben striking, and of a drive to Shannon Airport, through that no-man's-land which surrounds all airports, where trees, cows, and cottages, still strewn about the landscape, lose their relevance, and the progress over coarse grass and tarmac becomes a journey through time rather than space. Three people take this drive. At no time during the book have they been so portrayed as to suggest that any one of them is capable of taking in all the impressions recorded. But there sits in the car with them a kind of collective consciousness which perceives and records more than they do. This consciousness is sometimes specifically identified as 'one'. . . . When a plane appears, 'one watched its hesitating descent'. When Big Ben strikes, 'one was hearkening to an ultimatum'.

This is only permissible when *one* is an element in which all things, people, tarmac, clock strokes, exist like fish in a tank. The egocentric method is the very opposite of the Tolstoyan method, where each moment is limited by the perceptions of a single character.

'In silence they came to the table. The footmen drew out and pushed up the chairs. Pierre unfolded his cold dinner napkin and, making up his mind to break the silence, he glanced at Natasha and Princess Marya.'

The word *cold* commits the scene to Pierre, by emphasizing a sensation particular to him. There is no place for *one* here. The most profound and illuminating piece of perception would be a blunder unless it were his; when he passes on the record it will be to Natasha, Marya, or a footman. Yet it was at one time, not very long ago, possible for a writer to present some scene in the Tolstoyan manner and, at any moment, to interrupt it by some little cadenza of sensibility totally alien to the perceptions of anybody present. Such validity as the scene might have had is shattered, but this disaster was less likely to be noticed at a time when top marks were always given to any exhibition of sensibility.

In making a possible list for the attic these questions can be put: Why was the form chosen? Did it suit the material? Did the author appear to understand it? Had he the gifts required by those who use it? Is any departure from it deliberate, an experiment, or merely an indication that he did not perceive its limitations? Upon the answers will depend the sheer readability of the book in thirty years' time. Whether, even if readable, it will be read, is another matter. That depends upon content. He need not sign his own death-warrant in advance. If he does so sign it, however striking the content, to the attic he will go.

The passages quoted in this chapter are from the following books:

Pamela. Richardson.

Joseph Andrews. Fielding.

The Odyssey. Homer. Translated by E. V. Rieu.

The Old Wives' Tale. Bennett.

A World of Love. Bowen.

CHAPTER IX

Faking

Delacroix once said that an artist must always spoil a picture a little in order to finish it. This is a hard saying, but many novelists would be obliged to agree. Their material is always in peril of sustaining some irreparable damage during its transit from the imagined world to this one. It is volatile and perishable. Some part of it does not stand up to the rigours of the journey. What was conceived as a perfect whole arrives in harbour full of gaps. These gaps the writer must fill, as best he can. This damage he must repair, since it is his business to get his cargo into port somehow.

If he is lucky it is only a small disaster. Some minor character refuses to take life. A particular incident does not materialize in vivid detail.

Faking

An essential corner of the landscape remains dim and cloudy. He confidently asks: 'What sort of man was the Uncle? What trees grew in the orchard? What exactly happened when Mr. Jones fell off his horse?' No answer is forthcoming. The uncle, the orchard, and the horse are missing.

This unfortunate hiatus must be filled by invention, ingenuity, guess work, and by drawing upon experience in the raw, rather than upon that distilled essence of it which is the true cargo. He asks himself: 'What sort of man was the uncle likely to be? What trees might one expect to see in an orchard? What generally happens when a man falls off a horse?'

To send out for an uncle is easy enough. There are plenty of uncles about. He can be borrowed from the kitty, or drawn from life, from somebody known to the writer, and he can be groomed into a family resemblance to the other characters. Apple trees are a safe guess for an orchard. Information, useful for the Jones incident, can be collected from somebody who keeps a riding stables. The edges, between these fakes and the adjoining material, are smoothed over. For a time they exhibit a spurious life although they never came from that far country where uncles, orchards, and accidents are perceived as something strange, individual, and authentic.

It would appear that many readers never suppose a novelist to work in any other way; they do not credit him with an ounce of imagination. He must be prepared to be asked, to the end of his life, 'who Flora really was'. He may even be asked this by people who are paid to review fiction. Should he survive his period, research will be made into the originals of all his characters, all the orchards will be identified, and there will be a controversy as to when, exactly, he can have fallen off a horse. His warmest admirers will discuss his work as though it were nothing save a gigantic fake, a scrap-book of actual scenes, characters, and incidents, neatly put together.

There have doubtless been a few, a very few, writers who never faked. This is not because no disaster ever befell their cargo, but because they preferred to leave a gap, a blur, one figure faintly blocked in, rather than offer a substitute of different material. Jane Austen's Mary Bennet must have failed her at some point. She had conceived of five sisters, one of them a bluestocking, but the bluestocking did not turn up in very good shape. Mary is in a far lower state of finish than the other girls; even the nonentity Kitty has more impact. She is not very funny. Her creator preferred to leave her in this plight, although a faked bluestocking would have been the easiest thing in the world for a woman of such satiric wit to concoct. Miss Austen could have turned out a riotously funny Mary, had she chosen. She did not choose, and she was right, since the pseudo-Mary would, in the end, have done more harm to the book than the genuine, but substandard, Mary.

For there comes a time when the reader is aware of the difference in quality, he hardly knows why. He complains that the scenes with the uncle are dull and that Mr. Jones's accident never seems quite plausible. These patches of dead paint begin to annoy him. As a result he often complains that he is unconvinced by those passages in the book which have, actually, the most factual warrant. The writer, lacking the warrant of inner conviction, has taken great pains to secure authenticity of another sort.

Few admirers of Hardy find the suicide of Jude's children convincing, although he had chapter and verse for saying that such a thing could happen. The second Mrs. Hardy, in conversation with friends, confirmed the story that he saw a paragraph in the newspaper, describing just such an incident.

It was told of Edward Grey, who warmly admired Hardy, that his response to this book was to exclaim: 'It's not true, and Hardy knows it's not true!' He meant that Hardy did not really believe it about Jude's children, whatever the newspapers might say some other stonemason's children had done. The change in texture, colour, and climate, which overtakes the narrative, when the time comes for the children to hang themselves, is characteristic of an imaginative hiatus in the middle of a great book. Hardy, searching in his hold for the tragic climax, found nothing save an old newspaper cutting.

Most readers account for their discomfort over this episode by exclaiming that it is too dreadful! Too shocking! Actually they are aware that it is not nearly shocking enough; it is hurried over in the most perfunctory way. As often happens when a fake is necessary, Hardy begins to imitate himself. Jude and Sue talk too much and too sedulously in character. He quotes Aeschylus, and the inevitable irony comes in very pat when they are interrupted by a noise outside the window: two clergymen in the street are wrangling about the Eastward

138

Position. 'Good God—the Eastward Position, and all creation groaning!' The children are hurried into their grave. Sue's frantic scrabblings, her attempt to dig them up again, excite no genuine thrill of horror because they are merely an answer to the question: How would a mother, in such circumstances, be *likely* to behave? There is no shared pang, such as George Eliot communicates when Amos Barton returns to his parsonage after his wife's funeral. There she did not have to ask herself what he felt; she merely had to write down what she knew he saw—the blinds, which had for three days shrouded the house in a timeless twilight, all drawn up again; the cold empty rooms filled with the hard glare of snow reflected daylight; whereat time and change whispered their first dreadful message and he knew that he must meet them both alone.

Great writers have generally been bad fakers, since the difference in the quality of the material has been more difficult to disguise. George Eliot's *Daniel Deronda* is, for this reason, fascinating and unreadable almost in alternate chapters. She had been determined to write a novel about Jews and had got them up very thoroughly. But all the Jews died on the journey and nothing would bring them to life again, however accurately they might quote the Talmud. Had nothing survived the journey she must surely have abandoned the book. A good deal did survive: Gwendolen Harleth, Grandcourt Mallinger, Klesmer, Mrs. Glasher, the sooty Manor House among the collieries, no longer good enough for a wife but the very place for a mistress, and the four wary little bastards whose heads were 'duly patted' by their father, even though he only came to get back the diamonds which he had given to their mother when he liked her better. With such material, of course she had to write the book.

It would have been a great shame if she had given it up since the readable parts are so enthralling, nor is it easy to see how she could have dropped the Jews, even if she had wished to do so. Daniel Deronda himself is necessary to Gwendolen's story, and his wholehearted pre-occupation with the Jewish cause is necessary too. Her egotism is at its most formidable after she has, as children say, 'got good'. We have already seen her take a toss, in her unregenerate days, when Klesmer punctures her notion that she can retrieve the family fortunes by becoming an opera singer. Surprisingly, we have been forced, if not to feel sorry for her, at least to comprehend her bewilderment and sick

140

dismay as her young world comes tumbling down about her ears. It is one of George Eliot's major achievements that she can force us to scrutinize the sufferings of disagreeable people, who deserve all they get, quite as closely as we do the undeserved afflictions of the amiable. This early scene with Klesmer strikes a note for which we then wait, unconsciously, all through the book, until we hear it again in the final scene with Daniel. In many great novels there is this pattern: there are two scenes, one early and one late, both in the same key, and the second, for which the first has prepared the way, turns out to be all we feared and hoped it might. She expects Klesmer to tell her how to outshine Grisi. He advises her to take a post as governess in a Bishop's family. She expects Daniel to tell her how to be good. Once an egotist, always an egotist, she cannot suppose that he has any task in life save to guide her and tell her what is right. She worships him utterly, yet has never felt the least curiosity about his life and interests, save where they affect her own. He is as one-dimensional to her as Klesmer was. He dismisses her to a future of unapplauded virtue in the sooty Manor House; he is very sorry for her, but the Jewish cause is his task in life and he is off to Smyrna. This time her world

141

collapses for good. A full-length portrait of Daniel was necessary—a man who is wholly devoted to some great disinterested cause and who is kind to her, simply because it is his nature to be kind. But most of his personal story seems to be taking place, not in the land of the living, but in some Institute for Jewish Affairs.

There is a type of faking which is not so easily identified; it occurs when a writer of distinction, with an impressive record, exasperated by one of those sterile periods which all must endure, loses patience. He writes a book which might be called a Reputational Novel. He writes it simply because he thinks that his reputation demands another addition to literature. Against the grain he finishes some book which has been laid aside because the impetus subsided. Or he rips some imaginative concept from its chrysalis before it is ready for treatment. This book appears to be so very like his other books that his admirers can never quite account for their own lack of enthusiasm. It can truly be said that he has never written better; knowing in his heart that he ought not to be writing it at all, he takes the utmost trouble over it.

Faking

Examples of the Reputational Novel are not easy to name since they are the least often remembered, read, or quoted. Great novelists have generally possessed enough fortitude to eschew them; Jane Austen did so, in the case of *The Watsons*. The few which survive nearly always exhibit some traces of the genuine article—a hint of what the book might have been, had it survived, or had it been allowed to mature. Possible examples are: Burney's *Camilla*, Richardson's *Sir Charles Grandison*, Charlotte Brontë's *Shirley*, Conrad's *The Rover*, Wharton's *Hudson River Bracketed* and—Thackeray's *The Virginians?*

There is a contemporary form of faking peculiar to English novelists since 1945. It arises from the economic situation and may vanish when that situation alters. It might be called the Extra Currency Novel, and it is interesting because the faking can be so clearly discerned.

Novelists are allowed extra currency for foreign travel if they can say they need to travel in order to write. On the same ground they can put quite a substantial part of the cost of such travel into Professional Expenses, when making up their income tax returns. Many of them, on the strength of this, take a holiday in Ravenna or Mexico. A few are so very honest that they feel they ought to write a book about it as soon as they get home. Not to do so would be to cheat their Queen and their country and to make false statements on Inland Revenue forms.

Sometimes, of course, they really want to write this book and would have written it in any case. The new place visited has immediately set their imaginations alight. But there is no sure guarantee that this will happen, or that it will happen soon. Imaginative absorption can be amazingly rapid or amazingly slow, and there is no hurrying the process. The crucible will reject experiences which might have been expected to act as powerful stimulants, yet transmute trivial incidents, scarcely regarded at the time, into lasting treasure. A writer may live through an earthquake and never, to the end of his days, find anything to say about it; the spectacle of a dog fight in Hyde Park may unaccountably set him off.

The Extra Currency Novel gives a factual account of the author's trip. There is generally a good deal about food. The more naïve sometimes begin eagerly with the blue plates on the

144

train between Calais and Paris. There is some
moderate sight-seeing. The famous sights are
left alone, but there is often some little church,
or a fountain in some neglected piazza, about
which Baedeker has not already said everything. Into this travelogue are introduced
fictitious characters, eating the scampi or the
tortillas, peering at mosaics or discussing the
Aztecs. They have a livelier time, when they
retire for the night, than the honest author
probably did. A love-affair blows up, idyllic
enough to account for the high spirits which
pervade the trip, sad enough to harmonize with
the gloom in which we catch the homeward
plane.

Characters and setting are as incompatible as
though figures had been drawn on a coloured
picture post card. It is a phenomenon which
aptly illustrates the nature of faking and the
impossibility of exploiting experience in the
raw. In a genuine novel the landscape, down to
the last raindrop, the last blade of grass, went
through some process of transmutation before
it was used. Few landscapes could have less in
common than those of Kafka and Trollope,
but the same alchemy lies behind both. Were
it otherwise we should not still be reading
Barchester Towers.

145

This metamorphosis is understood in the neighbouring kingdom of poetry. The poets can put up pleasure domes in Xanadu without having been there; they can refer to 'the sole Arabian tree' without being brought to book by people who can tell them for a fact that there are lots of trees in Arabia. That the novelist's landscape is of the same quality is seldom allowed because it is less fantastic, and resembles more closely the readers' world. He does not denude Arabia of all trees save one; he does, in a lordly way, decree the exact number of trees which suit him best in any scene, whereas the 'reporter' is fettered by the actual number of trees in a given place, whether they be too many or too few. Values and qualities are subject to a myriad small changes and modulations; the importance of some is enlarged, of others diminished; the emphasis shifts; a deeper glow is added here, a darker shadow there; this horizon is brought nearer, that one is thrust away to a great distance.

All this he must do in order that Flora may have air to breathe, ground beneath her feet, and a bus to catch when she goes shopping. If he has to borrow a bus for her he weakens, in some degree, her essential quality. Her own bus so nearly resembles the reader's bus that

146

nobody, save perhaps another novelist, might locate the difference. Yet if she always rode in borrowed buses, the reader would know it. She would take no hold on him. He believes in her because everything which she sees, hears, smells, tastes, and touches, is of a piece with her. They are all part of the same cargo, whether the method employed is naturalistic, fantastic, prosaic, poetic, factual, or allusive.

That this is seldom understood is not surprising when so many people suppose that Flora herself has been borrowed. They are, moreover, convinced that the borrowing must have been done in the dreariest, the most humdrum way. Mr. L. W. Tancock, whose translation of *Manon Lescaut* is published by Penguin Books, adds a preface in which he gives a good deal of information about Prevost. He mentions the visit to England, 1728–30, the friends made there, and the probability that it was during those years that Prevost 'gathered his experience together' in order to write his sole masterpiece. What experience? Was there, speculates Mr. Tancock, a *real* Manon? Did she 'cross his path' during those two years? Of *Moll Flanders*, published some eight or nine years earlier, there is not a word, in spite of the identical titles, in spite of the similarity of subject, in spite of the alteration in style, which is, as Mr. Tancock points out, much simpler and more factual, much closer to beautiful bare narrative, than the other volumes of *Les Memoires et Aventures d'un Homme de Qualité qui s'est retiré du Monde*. The soaring excitement, the wild surmise, which one writer can inspire in another, is completely overlooked, although it is the influence most likely to exalt a minor artist to a level far beyond his normal capacities. Prevost, by all accounts, met all too many Manons in 'real life'. That he might have met one quite elsewhere is an experience only thought credible in a poet. Keats might go off like a rocket after looking into Chapman's Homer. If a novelist displays excitement, after reading a book, it can only be because he must have met some young woman in the book shop.

It is a fate to which he resigns himself. When asked who Flora really was he learns not to insist that he invented her. To do so will excite an obvious, if unuttered, suspicion that he met her in circumstances which do him no credit. He says that she was his great aunt, and remembers that Mrs. Florence Hardy was obliged to keep a list of the conflicting stories told by Hardy about 'the real Tess', in order that he might not mix them up. To be asked

148

the question is, moreover, a sign that Flora is thought of as *somebody*, even by these dunces. It is not inflicted upon the synthetic novelist in the same way. His Flora does not provoke so much curiosity, and, in any case, most people know who she was and that she is very angry about it. The question is not, of course, an indication that Flora will survive her creator, but it is evidence that she bears up very well.

CHAPTER X

'Anyway, I think so!'

There is no law against the didactic novel. Nothing forbids a writer so to frame his story as to sustain a moral, prove a theory, preach a Gospel, expose a fallacy, or advocate a reform. *What you can do you may do* obtains in this field of art as it does in all the others. Harriet Beecher Stowe could do it, and so could John Bunyan. There are indications that George Orwell may have done it. *Animal Farm* is already quoted by people who do not know the source; that is one of the signs that a book has taken root.

The vast majority of writers however are likely to come to grief if they attempt such a thing. Their art will suffer and their readers will be bored—disasters which coincide more

150

often than might be supposed. As far as they can, they would be wise to keep their personal opinions in the background.

A good many years ago a young man wrote a novel in order to show how badly he had been brought up, and how little a public school had done for him. In these objects he was so successful that his manuscript might not have got into print if it had been submitted three years earlier or three years later. It was offered soon after the publication of Alec Waugh's *The Loom of Youth*, when little victims were all the reading. A publisher could load up with any amount of them and hope to make a profit.

Although the material was autobiographical, impersonal narrative was chosen. It presented an imagined boy, sensitive, vulnerable, and brilliantly gifted, who was, at home, misunderstood, neglected, and deceived; at school, mocked, maltreated, and corrupted. At one point the author's grievances got the better of him. He broke off the narrative and introduced a tirade beginning with: 'One would have thought that parents . . .' and ending with: 'Anyway, *I* think so!'

This, in its crudest form, is an example of something which can chill and confuse the reader's response, even in a very great novel.

151

The author's personal opinions, beliefs, and canons of taste are bound to be reflected, strive though he may to keep them in the background. But they are acceptable to the reader only so long as they are not forced down his throat. He resents any suggestion that he is being asked to subscribe to them. He likes to be treated as a guest in the author's world, where he travels in complete personal liberty. He is taken everywhere, shown everything, but he does not relish a lecture about his own world, and an invitation to apply for naturalization may make him pack up and go home.

In a great novel some faint whisper of *I think so* can go through the whole fabric like an earthquake tremor. Tolstoi, just occasionally, abandons that exquisite technique, which he made so much his own, and which often seems to be the voice of humanity itself, for a lecture in some other voice, an alien scratchy voice, belonging to nobody present. Such a passage occurs when a visit to the opera plays its part in the downfall of Natasha. Tolstoi disliked Grand Opera. He thought it false and insincere, therefore morally corrupting. He describes this one with laboured sarcasm, with an affectation of incomprehension, as though some Choctaw, some visitor from the moon,

had got into the theatre and understood nothing
that he saw.

'In the second act there was scenery repre-
senting monuments, and a hole in the drop
at the back that represented the moon, and
shades were put over the footlights, and
trumpets and bassoons began playing, and a
number of people came in on the right and on
the left wearing black cloaks. These people
began waving their arms, and in their hands
they had something in the nature of a dagger.
Then some more people ran in and began
dragging away the woman who had been in
white but who was now in a blue dress. They
did not drag her away at once: they spent a
long while singing with her: but finally they
did drag her away, and behind the scenes they
struck something metallic three times, and
then all knelt down and began singing a prayer.
All these performances were interrupted
several times by the enthusiastic shouts of the
spectators.'

This does not, at first, chill the reader, since
it might be Natasha's opera. We are told that
she saw it like this and found it both grotesque
and false. Later we learn that she was 'completely under the spell of the world in which
she now found herself. All that passed before

her eyes now seemed perfectly natural.' In this case it has ceased to be Natasha's opera since she sees it differently. Somebody, however, continues to see it as grotesque and false. This Choctaw continues his petulant description through act after act, in paragraphs which interrupt and confuse the account of what is happening to Natasha, her increasing pre-occupation with Anatole in the next box, her surrender to an evil spell.

It is an element of arrogance and egotism in it which trips up the artist and repels the reader. This element is absent in the great didactic novels; there is none of it in *Uncle Tom's Cabin*, or in *Pilgrim's Progress*. These authors did not write in order to tell us what they think, but to serve some cause which seemed to them sublime and in which all thought of self was lost. Such passionate humility, combined with creative gifts, will sometimes preserve the didactic novelist; it will capture readers who have no particular sympathy with the cause, or who regard it as a battle fought and won a long time ago.

It is perhaps for this reason that the works of Charlotte Yonge were not only admired by discriminating readers in her own day, but are still read with pleasure by a small, but not unintelligent, public. Her didacticism must have demolished her had she ever evinced the least trace of personal arrogance or conceit. She wrote in support of the Oxford Movement, to which cause her life was dedicated, and from whence she derived her ethical code. She is too highminded to reward the good with more than peace of mind and, not infrequently, an early death. But no misdeed, not the smallest peccadillo, escapes retribution. Agnostic governesses give their pupils brain fevers. Flirtation over the croquet hoops is lethal. Death in a decline awaits village schoolmistresses who read Shelley. Those who neglect the rite of Confirmation fall a prey to melancholia thirty years later. Any truck with Dissenters invariably leads, not to one, but to a series of catastrophes.

Yet—she is still read! She is read for the sake of her undeniable merit. She was born with great natural gifts, with a superb creative vitality, which might have taken her to the very top of the ladder had she subjected those gifts to the discipline imposed by an artist's conscience. She is a literary casualty, not because she was didactic, but because this conscience had, by her creed, to be kept in a straight waistcoat. She really believed that Eve gave the apple to Adam, and that the complete

155

subjection of women is a punishment which they must accept with resignation until Judgement Day. She obeyed other people all her life, thus denying herself experiences and information which she needed for her work. As a child she was forbidden to go into a cottage; she observed this interdict till the day of her death. She shut her mind when told to do so, and an unmarried woman, at that time, was often so instructed. One of her heroines, Eustacie de Ribaumont in *The Chaplet of Pearls*, gives the reader as great a start as ever Meredith's Carinthia did, for the same reason; no examination of the text can explain the miracle. She wrote too much and too fast, and she sent all her earnings to foreign missions. She conscientiously refrained from taking too much trouble over her work since she had been told that this might tempt her to pride and vanity; it must never be 'an end in itself'.

It is for these reasons that she survives among the minor Victorians, not the major. What she would have written, had her other conscience been given rope, is a matter for fascinating speculation. The modifications might have been very slight; perhaps they would have been almost imperceptible save to the connoisseur of the novel. Less would have

156

been written. More time would have been allowed for incubation, musing, cutting, pondering, and revision. The result would have been less diffuse and repetitive, the canvases less crowded. She would still however have been didactic, since she was a born enthusiast. She would have carried a gun for somebody. It was a misfortune for literature that she carried a gun for Keble.

The perils of didacticism in religion, politics and ethics are pretty commonly understood and avoided. Inadvertent slips are rare save in inexperienced writers. In the region of aesthetics, where the going is quite as tricky, the pitfalls are less plainly charted. The writer's *I think so* about art, taste, and culture may very easily get him into trouble.

The Author-Observer has the same advantage here that he has when he is describing Fanny bursting through her stays. He can state his own preferences since he is admittedly on the scene, and can allow that they are his own. This gives the reader liberty to disagree. The impersonal narrator must beware lest he should have the air of setting up some standard of taste which ought to be universally accepted.

157

There is a scene in *Vanity Fair* where Becky sings Mozart's religious music to Lady Steyne. It might be made the text for several debates upon the treatment of art in a novel. Thackeray made no secret of his enthusiasm for Mozart. He believed that this composer has the power to bring out the best in everybody, and when he wanted to give his characters a treat he sent them to *Don Giovanni*. Becky sang:

'With such sweetness and tenderness that the lady, lingering round the piano, sate down by its side, and listened until the tears rolled down her eyes. It is true that the opposition ladies at the other end of the room kept up a loud and ceaseless buzzing and talking: but Lady Steyne did not hear these rumours. She was a child again and had wandered back through a forty years wilderness to her convent garden. The chapel organ had pealed the same tones: the organist, the sister whom she loved best of the community, had taught them to her in those happy early days. She was a girl once more, and the brief period of her happiness bloomed out again for an hour. She started when the jarring doors were flung open, and, with a loud laugh from Lord Steyne, the men of the party entered full of gaiety.

'He saw at a glance what had happened in his

absence, and was grateful to his wife for once. He went and spoke to her, and called her by her Christian name, so as again to bring blushes to her pale face.'

Realists would have a sizeable bone to pick with Thackeray about all this. The date is apparently about 1820. How much of Mozart's religious music would have been, with any likelihood, heard in a convent garden forty years earlier, was a point which never troubled a writer of his generation. Mozart was alive in 1780, which was good enough. Only a pedant would inquire into the number of his religious compositions at that date, and the probability of their being performed outside the German churches by which they had been commissioned. Thackeray never hesitated to bestow upon his regency characters the views, tastes, opinions, language, and sometimes the clothes, of 1848. A strict realist would find this shocking; a good artist, he would say, must know exactly what music made Lady Steyne cry so much. The scene otherwise is false, because insufficiently imagined. The tedium and triviality of the Italian music most likely to have been favoured in a convent in 1780 ought not to harm the effect. A good writer should be able to convey the same pathos whatever rubbish

159

Becky happened to be singing; it would, in fact, be a stronger scene if she *was* singing rubbish. It ought not to depend upon any borrowed magic; it should not drag in the writer's, or the reader's, idea of good music.

And supposing, say the debaters on the other side, supposing Thackeray had got it all up, would he have achieved his object any better? Would he, indeed, have done as well? The reader is moved. Would evidence that the author is a very knowing fellow, never out in his facts, intensify the pathos? Would it not have been most unwise of Thackeray, in 1848, to associate pathos with a kind of music not yet quite forgotten but generally derided? A vogue sixty years old has still too many associations for the living, and these are not sympathetic. A writer today, wishing to convey the power of poetry, would be imprudent to choose Browning. Any other poet would be safer. There are still too many readers for whom Browning spells the voiceless rebellions of their childhood, and memories of *Saul*, read aloud by their parents in hushed tones on Sunday evenings. In another fifty years Browning will probably be as safe as Herrick.

These are some of the snares which lie in wait for the writer who mentions art. They are

nothing to those which attend the actual presentation of artists. To venture upon an artist
as a major character is a bold undertaking,
especially if it is to be suggested that he is a good
artist. Some indication must be given of the
kind of work he does. It will not do to say that
all stood in awe before this magnificent canvas
without a hint of what was to be seen on it. The
writer will naturally furnish his own notion of
a good picture. Should the reader have some
other notion he will think that these awe-
struck spectators had no taste. A poet hero is
even more formidable. Sooner or later some
specimens of his verse will have to be quoted;
the writer will have to make these up himself.
An outburst of applause from the characters in
the book will do nothing to convince the reader
that these lines display genius. Nor is it wise,
if the poet be contemporary, to assert that a
favourable verdict was passed by 'the critics'.
What? thinks the reader. Must I really believe
that Messrs. Mortimer, Pritchett, Empson, etc.,
were all beside themselves with admiration
over this rubbish? The author must create his
own critics, bring them onto the stage, and
make them say why they admire the work. The
reader may decide that they had no taste, but
his credulity will not be strained to snapping

161

point. If the author's world provides art, it must also provide criticism.

One solution is to borrow the productions of some well known artist. In *The Moon and Sixpence* Mr. Maugham gives us to understand that his hero has painted pictures to which Gauguin would have owned any day, and then dares anyone to say that Gauguin could not paint. It is a good solution as long as this artist, borrowed as a backer, keeps up his reputation. A much-admired Victorian novel, E. S. Sheppard's *Charles Auchester*, borrowed Mendelssohn in the same way, got into Dent's *Everyman's Library*, and kept up bravely as long as Mendelssohn kept up. Nor will this solution do for the poet hero, for there are still those quotations. If we are to understand that he writes Dr. T. S. Eliot's verse for him, some half-dozen lines will have to be quoted, at some point, which would be undetectable if inserted into *The Waste Land*.

Some writers have ventured on such a task, but not many. Kipling, in *Dayspring Mishandled*, offers some synthetic Chaucer which, he asserts, deceived a Chaucerian expert. This is no great risk, since the expert is something of a charlatan. But Kipling also suggests that the whole human race is likely to be deceived, a possibility which no reader has been able to swallow.

The only safe course is to follow the example of Petronius, who used a method whereby any novelist can express his personal opinions, upon art or anything else, and even quote his own verse, in perfect safety. Petronius had very strong opinions about art, which he made no attempt to conceal. He gives them all to Eumolpus, a disgraceful old thimble rigger, the seediest character in the *Satyricon*. It is Eumolpus who makes that pregnant remark about Myron. He is also credited with a couple of poems which have puzzled some scholars by their elegance and distinction. All the other characters throw stones at Eumolpus when he insists upon reciting his poetry, and they make him take a vow to write no more. He is eventually flung into the sea in very undignified circumstances.

Scholars, after nearly two thousand years, are still wondering why Petronius gave this verse, and these opinions, to Eumolpus. J. M. Mitchell, describing the poems as 'admirable in technique and in execution and a real contribution to the poetry of the early Imperial period', says:

'Are we then to imagine that Petronius

163

meant them to be taken as serious compositions? If so, why does he put them into the
mouth of an absurd character like Eumolpus?
On the other hand, it is Eumolpus who talks so
well about art. . . . It is a great puzzle.'*

Had the novel ever received the kind of close
study accorded to poetry, the puzzle might not
have been so great. Petronius may well have
had a very high opinion of his own verse. As
an accomplished novelist he knew a great deal
better than to say so.

* Petronius. The *Satyricon* translated by J. M. Mitchell.

CHAPTER XI

Ethics

The reader who expects to find his own ethical code endorsed in a novel is not the kind of reader with whom Lamb's implied compact must be kept, for he is a stupid creature. He takes a trip abroad, into the author's world, and then complains that it is not a home from home. The people are funny; they speak another language; they eat snails; they drive on the wrong side of the road and they do not know that pillar-boxes ought to be painted red.

Desirable readers do not make this kind of complaint. They may dislike the journey so much that they never return, but they do not expect Xanadu to put them in mind of Yarmouth. They do, however, like to know the rate of exchange in the local ethical currency. They will accept a novel in which Judas Iscariot is the blue-print for a good man, so long as they know where they are. They want ethics: not necessarily their own, but ethics of some sort. In a story of the underworld told by a jail-bird, a Moll Flanders, they need not be at a loss. The narrator may have no ethics, but they know how his world rates him; it treats him as a miscreant although he, personally, has never been able to understand why. It is not in crime stories that a reader is most likely to lose his way. That is more liable to happen if he finds himself among people who have kept out of Wormwood Scrubs but who do not seem to be aware of any difference between right and wrong. He wants to know what kind of man these natives would recognize as good, what kind of actions they would condemn as bad.

To present a very good man is a formidable task for any writer. The difficulties were summed up by Agatha Christie, who complained that an honest man has been described as the noblest work of God, and that to turn one out, once a year, in time for the Autumn List, is to engage in august competition. Imagined as a saint he has dwindled into a prig or a simpleton by the time that he has been got down on to paper. His thoughts and motives do not, after all, seem to be quite worthy of him.

It is not a task often undertaken by the egocentrics, although Elizabeth Bowen took the risk, with Major Brutt, in *The Death of the Heart*. For most egocentrics it involves too much inquiry into the external. The essential material cannot be located by 'looking within'. Contact with a genuinely good man does not leave us with the impression that he is exactly like ourselves, only better; that the difference lies merely in the fact that he makes more frequent, more effective, struggles to do right, and sits more sternly upon his lower self. He exists upon some other level. The process is not quite the same. He is like a very good tennis player who frightens a bad tennis player by driving past a child playing hopscotch on the pavement without putting on his brakes. At the suggestion that the child might have hopped under the car he says calmly that she could not do so because she was on the wrong foot. The bad tennis player suddenly perceives that his tennis is not tennis at all to the other. For him it is a matter of a ball which comes at him over a net and which he must try to hit. For the other it is a matter of the foot on which his opponent stands when he sends his own ball over. An expert, in some activity in which we have amateurishly dabbled, will often give us a surprise of this sort. He is not merely doing what we do, and doing it much better. He thinks of the whole thing quite differently. A very good man sometimes gives us the impression that he has gone a long way beyond ethics and scarcely needs them. He does not seem to know that he is good. What else could I have done? he says, in genuine surprise. He has not gone through that process of struggle and debate in which we would have engaged if we had so acted; the very fact that he has not done so forbids us to call him a prig. It is a mystery which we cannot hope to penetrate if we merely inquire within.

The genuinely good often provoke us to laughter, in spite of our respect for them. The simplicity of their outlook takes us by surprise. In 1940 a man, possessing the virtue of enormous natural courage, was telling his wife what to do in case of invasion. Should strangers come to the house at night, when he was out with the Home Guard, she must demand their credentials before giving them any information. She objected that, if they were really the enemy, they might shoot her unless she complied. To this he gave some consideration and then said:

168

'I don't think that would matter. Out in the country it might be wiser to stall until you could give the alarm. But in a built-up area like this the shot would be heard. Why on earth are you laughing?'

This background of laughter may explain why a good man has often been very well done by prosaic, unambitious writers with a pretty realistic technique and a strong turn for comedy. Nobody has ever called Trollope's Mr. Harding a prig, or doubted his genuine goodness, as he saws away on an imaginary 'cello and perceives that he has no alternative save to resign the wardenship of Hiram's Hospital. The 'cello, like Elsie's umbrella, is a convincing little bit of detail. Such a feat does not require any great preoccupation with ethics. It does imply some understanding of the impact which genuine goodness makes upon the average man; a writer who does not check his own impressions by those accumulated in the common stock is less likely to achieve it.

Novelists are sometimes reproached by their friends for never supplying the world with a hero whom all can respect and admire. Why do they fill their books with so-so characters, against the most estimable of whom there is a good deal to be said? The plea that a good man is very difficult to present is received with polite incredulity. It should surely be easy! Let all his actions be admirable, all his thoughts noble, and the thing is done! Yet, if they got him, these malcontents would complain that he is not convincing. George Orwell solved the problem by following Swift's example. He bestowed all the human virtues—faith, courage, patience, self-sacrifice, loyalty, humility, dignity—upon a very good horse.

An outstandingly bad man, on the other hand, is not easy material, if he is to be three-dimensional. He generally appears merely as the villain of the piece, as a mechanical contrivance, and as soon as he is foiled he is done with. To present him entire is not within the power of every writer. The yard-stick of ethics will not altogether measure him; he is not exactly like ourselves, only worse. He also may have a different way of looking at things.

A strong degree of detachment is valuable in his presentation. Those writers have dealt with him best who have been immensely interested in ethics, to whom good and bad are important ideas, but who have no particular case to present; for them the subject is eternally open to

170

debate. It was this detachment which enabled
Thackeray to do so well with Barry Lyndon.
Thackeray was something of a debater. He had
not the settled, the taken-for-granted, moral
code of many Victorians; he had no case to
make. When Becky thinks that she could have
been a good woman on five thousand a year and
ascribes Lady Jane's virtue to 'the influence of
a long course of Three per Cents' her creator
suggests that she was very likely right.

This detachment was not congenial to the
age and Thackeray was, avowedly, not the man
to quarrel with his age. This was very cynical,
and reveals him as a naughty boy to those who
believe that good boys invariably flay their age.
But it was this detachment, this disinclination
to quarrel with, or to flay, anybody, which
enabled him to do so well with Barry Lyndon
and Becky Sharp.

Charlotte Brontë hoped for more of him than
he could give, when she refused to class him
with Fielding and likened him to an eagle. She
was, herself, no debater. At variance with the
conventional ethics of the period, she wished to
have the debate opened for long enough to discover new, and more acceptable, premises. She
hoped that Thackeray would demolish false
virtues by presenting a landscape in which true

ones were implicit. Those in search of some categorical imperative will often make this mistake about debaters; they will confuse argument with advocacy. Had he been the eagle she thought him she might not have cared for the region into which such eagles soar. The great debaters, who have probed deeply into good and evil, have travelled with humanity from the heights to the depths, can never satisfy those who demand some final verdict. Thackeray stands at one end of the scale, with a smiling question, Dostoievsky at the other, with a shattering demand, but it is far from certain that Charlotte Brontë would have welcomed *Crime and Punishment*.

English novelists have not often joined in the debate. Joyce Cary, a recent debater, was an Irishman. Conrad wrote in English but he never thought like an Englishman. This gave him, at one time, a reputation for being more intelligent than he really was. He debated ably, but at no remarkable level. When *Lord Jim* appeared, with its counterpoint of various human verdicts, each dictated by circumstance, the originality of such an approach created an impression that it must be very profound. A civilized dinner-party conversation in one country will often produce such an impression upon a visiting stranger from another. The novelty in topic and approach strike him as evidence of extreme intelligence. Conrad's little French captain, whose verdict on Jim had to be what it was since he was a sailor and a Frenchman, evoked much admiring comment. To a generation accustomed to the debate at the level to which Cary raised it, fraught with the passion he imparted, Conrad's reputation, forty-five years ago, is an enigma.

It is the debaters who have done best with very bad men. Those with a case to present have been too much frightened of them, too much inclined to push them beyond the frontiers of humanity.

An implicit, simple, fairly commonplace ethical outlook is a great attraction in a writer, if he has it by nature. It imparts ease, confidence, and authority, which are the more powerful because they are unconsciously exerted. Writers enjoying such an outlook have not been very much interested in ethics as debatable ground. Questions of conduct engage them. The underlying ideas of right and wrong remain unchallenged and a very simple test will suffice in moments of doubt.

Scott had this kind of serviceable moral currency, and it is one which has been recognized in many periods, by many races. To him the test was the kept promise, the observed obligation; perfidy was the abominable thing. Trollope had it. Fielding had it. A sense of its presence has much to do with our calm pleasure in reading Turgenev. Dickens had it, in spite of a controversial style. Now that the horses he flogged are mostly dead, that debtors' prisons have gone the way of workhouses and uninspected schools, it can be perceived that his moral outlook was very simple. The distinction between right and wrong never gave him much trouble. 'Right Reverends and Wrong Reverends of every sort' were the villains. The machinations of a Quilp or a Monks are feeble and puny compared with the evils arising from the callousness of the godly. Humanity and compassion are his test. He rarely depicted a situation in which human kindness might not prevail. To have a good heart is everything. In thinking this he was by no means at loggerheads with his age; the flaying was not very savage and made nobody feel uncomfortable.

Jane Austen's outlook had the same sort of instinctive ethical stability in five out of the

174

six great books. In *Mansfield Park* it is shaken, as though she was aware of a challenge and of a case to be maintained. She is concerned to show that manners and morals are not identical and that it is dangerous to confuse them. Her letters reveal that she was, at the time, anxious over the upbringing of a family of motherless nephews and nieces. Lady Bridges, the grandmother in charge, did not always see eye to eye with Chawton. The manners of these children were receiving careful polish. Were they being taught 'to feel as they ought?' Might they not turn out 'good for nothing?' These children were so near to her heart that she could not treat the question lightly, or turn it to comedy. It is the only novel of the six in which real misfortune overtakes misdoers. Lydia and Wickham were good for nothing but we leave them in excellent spirits. General Tilney, Lucy Steele, and Mrs. Clay are all allowed to prosper in their own fashion.

This kind of tolerance is one of the attractions of a stable moral outlook. Writers possessing it are not on the defensive to justify their principles; they assume that most sensible people will agree with them. They can accept without fuss the obvious fact that the wicked frequently have the devil's own luck, are never brought to book, are not even noticeably racked by remorse. This has been so since Adam was turned out of Eden and must be accepted like the weather. Good is good, bad is bad, just the same, as everybody knows. Villains in their stories may be foiled, the good arrive at a reasonable degree of felicity, but this is presented as an agreeable turn of fortune, not as the fulfilling of a moral law. Trollope leaves us in no doubt as to his opinion of Mr. Slope; a face-slapping and the mockery of the Signora are the worst calamities which befall this odious creature. He is last heard of as doing very well and perhaps more likely to be happy, in his odious way, than is 'good' Mr. Arabin.

Writers today are sometimes abused for not possessing this confident, easy, good-natured authority. No man can assume it if he has not got it by nature, and, in this century, it is not easily acquired. The inherited traditional code, upon which it was generally founded, has gone into the melting pot. The very terms in which it was stated have now lost credit. The old school tie is a joke. A gentleman's agreement is an ambiguity. A divorced woman is not now automatically *déclassée*. There is no reason to suppose that every man has not still got his own code, as he always had. It is the labels which have been removed. The average man is less likely today, than he was at other periods, to suppose that his personal code will be generally accepted and understood. He is therefore inclined to advance it with diffidence; if he does so, he feels that a case must be made out for it. This, for a novelist, brings in its train the risk of didacticism, the peril of '*I* think so'.

In order to avoid this peril some writers endeavour to eliminate ethics altogether from the landscape of their books. So far as they are able they present nothing in terms of right or wrong. No characters are to be disturbed by the intrusion of the word *ought*. This secures the writer from moral didacticism but it can sometimes bewilder his readers. They feel that an element in normal human experience is missing. They doubt, as they would doubt, if nobody in the book took any form of nourishment. They do not want to know what these people have for dinner, but validity is shaken if it appears that nobody ever eats at all.

The same thing happens when characters, presented as normal specimens, not as candidates for Broadmoor, do not seem to have anything amongst them which might pass for a

177

conscience. In ordinary experience everyone has something of the sort; those who have very little often testify to ethics by expecting a good deal of it in other people. The word *ought* is constantly on their lips when complaining of their neighbours. Indeed those writers who eliminate ethics, not out of caution but on principle, believing right and wrong to be symbols of involuntary behaviour patterns, can talk in a very old-fashioned way about behaviour patterns which have caused them personal inconvenience. The language in which they describe the dishonesty of their agents, the sloth and avarice of their publishers, the cowardice, cruelty, and callousness of their friends, is just the kind of language which readers would recognize and welcome in their books. It would restore a missing landmark.

No writer can wish his readers to feel that they have lost their way. It is always his hope and intention that they shall be taking the desired trip without debate or question, thinking, feeling, perceiving this thing and that thing, in a designed succession, to a designed degree of intensity. If, by any means in his power, he can obtain this response, he will never willingly check it. Should he eliminate all familiar landmarks, offer a terrain in which all rivers appear to flow uphill, he sets himself a very hard task. He can make such an attempt, if he believes that success is within his power, but, before he decides to eliminate ethics, he would be wise to ask himself whether he is gifted enough to do without them. Has he indeed a vehicle so powerful that he can transport his passengers to the mountains of the moon? If he has not, he may run into worse trouble than that which he hoped to avoid. The reader, irritated by ethics unskilfully handled, may falter on the road. Bewildered by their disappearance he may refuse to take the trip at all: nor will he listen to the plea that he went uncomplainingly to the moon with X and Y. *What you can do you may do.* X and Y can do it. Z cannot because, poor fellow, he was behind the door when certain gifts were handed out.

CHAPTER XII

Author! Author!

The classic Convention of Dignity may have withheld the novel, as we know it, from the Greeks until Xenophon, who was in revolt against Atticism, wrote the *Cyropaedia*. It did not, however, withhold *The Odyssey*, which may be written in the form of an epic poem but is otherwise so like a novel that novelists have some right to exhibit it in their gallery. Homer, in the course of it, does everything which they have to do, and he disposes of their central problem with an ease which must wring a sigh of envy and admiration from all of them. The incompatible functions of narrative and creation cause him no distress. As creator, he is not there. He has achieved an anonymity so complete that, as Professor Phillimore puts it, repeated calls of: *Author! Author!* down the centuries, have failed to bring him before the curtain. *

He makes no comment. He reveals himself in no chats with the reader, no displays of sensitive perception, no choicely selected adjectives and epithets designed to deliver a personal signature. He tells a story. He sticks to facts. His power lies in the arrangement of these facts, the order in which they are narrated, and in all which he did not think it necessary to say. He never states a fact which the reader might be expected to infer for himself.

To this factual narrative the reader can give whatever response he pleases. He can take it in the way which affords him most delight. No story has given more delight, has evoked a richer variety of response, for the best part of three thousand years. This complete liberty allowed to men, to make what they like of it, sprang from a superb respect for the human understanding; it bestows upon the reader a sense of his own dignity, as though some great Prince were, without question, treating him as an equal. No writer can do this unless he is himself of royal stature, but the humblest

* *The Greek Romances*, J. S. Phillimore.

181

successor of Homer may write the better for recognizing that respect. However modest his little story, however lowly he may rate his own powers, such recognition will bring him into a more exalted conception of his art and his public.

Homer had two advantages which few later novelists have enjoyed. He was spared the difficult task of announcing that his characters existed. They were not a set of people of whom nobody had ever heard before; as entities already in the public mind he took them over from legends and earlier poems. He had the second advantage of addressing the most intelligent, the most subtle people ever known in the western world. Close contact with minds which approximate, in this rare degree, to his own best mind imaginable, will enable an artist to strip his work down to the barest essentials in a way which makes work, produced at other periods, look vulgarly ornate. It was probably only to such a public that so austere a form of the novel as a purely factual story could have been offered.

It is a popular misconception to think of *The Odyssey* as a travel story—as a series of episodes and adventures strung together on the character of the hero. This notion of it is so pre-

valent that any travel story is now likely to be
called an Odyssey. In lesser hands that is probably what Homer's story would have been,
since he must have got his material in that
shape. But it is not a narrative of events in
their time sequence, passing from one episode
to another, from the fall of Troy to the return
to Ithaca. Only five of the twenty-four books
are concerned with the travels of Odysseus.
The scene, in fifteen of them, is laid in Ithaca;
the last twelve cover a few days in time. One,
in which Odysseus does not appear, takes us to
Sparta. The remaining three tell of his sojourn
with the friendly Phaeacians.

In rescuing the material from its earlier
episodic shape Homer makes use of a variety of
narrative forms, changing from one to another,
according to the facts to be related. There is
always some technical reason for these changes.
He tells most of it in person, but the traveller's
tale he hands over to his hero, who entertains
the Phaeacians with an account of some of his
adventures since the fall of Troy. The reason
for this is obvious: autobiography deals best
with material covering many years and tricky
time lapses. Only one of these adventures has
Homer kept in his own hands; the episode with
Calypso; her offer of immortality and an escape

from all further peril, hardship and disappointment; her guest's refusal. Again the reason is obvious: Homer wished to give fuller particulars of that affair that Odysseus was likely to recount to the Phaeacians. A snub to a goddess was not a thing about which so prudent a man would have cared to say much.

The conventional travel story does not begin until the ninth book, after the main theme has been well established. This theme is not of travel but of return. As it is expanded, book by book, one of the most universal and ironic circumstances in human existence is gradually revealed: the complete disappearance of a man's place in the world as soon as he is dead, or believed to be dead. The gap made in the social fabric closes up like a hole in water. It must be so, if the human race is to survive. However much he has been loved, however sincerely he may be mourned, society must do without him. The survivors may piously declare that nobody can ever take his place or do what he did. Somebody must and will do so. Should he return, there would be no room for him. Of this ironic truth men have always, in all lands, among all races, been aware. Primitive people fear the spirits of the dead and take precautions against their attempts to return and their fury at knowing their place to be gone. Even the Christian burial service is full of comforting assurances that they will not embarrass us by coming back.

This theme of the dead man's return is not immediately announced. The story opens with a simple survey of the practical difficulties which await Odysseus should he ever get back to Ithaca. It suits a great many people to believe him dead. The first hint is in the hesitations, the frustration, of Telemachus. He, by nature active and energetic, does not know what to do because he does not know how to think of himself. Must he, in his thoughts, keep a place open for a man who may one day return to claim it? Or should he think and act as a dead man's son? From there, step by step, the story advances to the point when Odysseus stands in the dawn on the threshold of his house, praying for some voice from the living to call him back. It sweeps on to the great bow, unstrung since he sailed for Troy, and the thing which no man after him has been able to do.

In several places narrative is handed over to minor characters; that entrusted to Menelaus in the fourth book is of particular technical interest. Dr. Rieu, in the preface to his translation, mentions the possibility that, in the earlier material, there were two great travellers:

Menelaus and Odysseus. If this is so, we have a striking instance of the way in which a great artist will abide by an old convention yet twist it to suit a new purpose. Menelaus certainly tells a travel story, but with what a difference! There can be no complaint of monotonous repetition, or of two men telling about the same sort of thing in the same sort of way.

According to Chapman, Menelaus was, even in *The Iliad*, an ineffably comic character. Chapman also maintains that his stock epithet, *good*, is always particularly introduced when he is doing or saying something unusually absurd. Agamemnon calls a council to which he does not invite his boring younger brother. *Good* Menelaus comes all the same. Only a very good man would have complained, as he did, that the Trojans had ravished his wife in the flower of her youth and beauty, *without cause*.

'When,' asks Chapman, 'should a man play such a part but then? As though lovers looked for more cause in their love-suits than the beauties of the beloved; or that men were made cuckolds only for spite or revenge of some wrong precedent. But indeed Menelaus' true simplicity is this: to think that harms should not be done without harms foregoing . . . maketh him well deserve his epithet *agathos*.'

186

In *The Odyssey*, Telemachus visits Menelaus in order to ask a single question: Can you give me any news of my father? It takes the good king half the evening to say that he can. He has first to get over his shocked surprise at the bad behaviour of the suitors. He must then tell the history of his own travels; it is as though Homer, at this early point in the story, was deliberately laughing at the conventional traveller's tale. Menelaus is that type of globe-trotter whom we have all met. There are people who have a knack of making the most wonderful experiences sound rather dull and who are always most struck at their own resourcefulness in avoiding, not danger, but discomfort. (*Luckily we had remembered to bring the mosquito cream!*) Menelaus, obliged to hide among some seals, would have found the stench very disagreeable if he had not been provided with some ambrosia to put up his nostrils. He is not a whit the wiser for all his travels. It could never have been said of him that he came home '*plein d'usage et raison*'. Paris, Hector, Achilles, Agamemnon—all are dead. This sole survivor of the Trojan wars, untroubled by memory or foreboding, is chatting himself into a green old age. He has brought back with him simply that which he

187

set out to get; by his side sleeps Helen, for whom so many have lost their lives. The sun has set on the heroic age. *More geese than swans now live, More fools than wise.* Are none left? None? It is in this mood that we come to book five and to the last of the heroes. Odysseus now makes his appearance, a captive on Calypso's isle.

The Iliad and *The Odyssey* differ, not in form, but in the territory which they command. *The Iliad*, as Dr. Rieu points out, occupies those regions which were later taken over by Tragedy and the Drama. *The Odyssey* explores that middle kingdom between comedy and tragedy, which is the novelists' ground and which has been taken over by them. They can say many things which could not be said nearly so well, if at all, in any other medium. They can employ material which is outside the scope of the drama or the epic poem. Many of Homer's points might be called a novelist's points.

In the great fight with the suitors the characters of four men are revealed and sustained simultaneously, without taking off from the excitement and tension of the whole battle. The two slaves who fight shoulder to shoulder with

188

Odysseus and Telemachus are sharply differentiated. The leisurely pace, the roomy scope, of the novel has allowed us to learn much about the swineherd. A king's son in his own land, kidnapped and sold into slavery as a very little child, he loved Odysseus' sister, long ago when he was young. As boy and girl they had grown up together and he had hardly known himself a slave until they married Ctimene to a husband in Same. Her mother, too kind and tactful to give the forlorn boy one of her slaves to wife, sent him out of the house, with some new clothes, to work on the farm. He has not married and has made a little kingdom of his profession as a lonely man will, who has loved above his station rather than his deserts. He speaks of Ctimene as though he had never since seen a woman who could hold a candle to her; the whole of his devotion is given to her family and to his pigs. He has built twelve lordly sties for the sows, surrounded by a wall of quarried stone with a wild pear hedge on the top, and an extra stockade of split oak. He has trained four dogs to guard them. He rules the under-herds with good-natured efficiency; at night they sleep by the fire while he sleeps outside, in order to keep an eye on the porkers. For the goat-herd, who loafs about the town and

189

leaves his flock to underlings, he has a boundless contempt. His lot has been hard but he
does not think so. When Odysseus comes in
disguise to his hut, with a sad story to tell, he
gives his own in exchange, remarking that if a
man has been through much, and travelled far,
he begins in the end to enjoy his own memories,
even though they are sad ones. His place in the
fight is perfectly clear: he is serving the family.

For the cowman it is the adventure of a life-
time. He feels none of the tension and anxiety
endured by the others; he enjoys every moment
of it. They may deal out blows in grim silence;
he fights with a gleeful running comment:

'You foul-mouthed son of a braggart, I'll
teach you to control your fatuous tongue and
not to talk so big, but to leave judgement to the
gods, who are far wiser than you. Take that
in return for the cow's hoof you gave King
Odysseus when he begged in the hall.'

Such a speech has already parted company with the epic poem. It is too homely
and takes off from the heroic quality of the
fight. On the stage it would get a laugh at
the wrong moment. That great hazard, even
when tragedy and comedy were no longer rigidly
divided, forced upon the drama a hard and fast
distinction which rules out certain truths.

190

The response which the stage can evoke is far stronger and more absolute than that obtained by any novel, but it is limited by the fact that a theatre audience can only see, hear, and respond to, one thing at a time. The number of notes struck in a great play can be so many and so varied, that they give an impression of extreme complexity; they are, on analysis, a succession of single notes. When Shakespeare wished to show the mind of a king, and the minds of his soldiers, before a battle, he had to do so in successive scenes. Privates Bates, Court, and Williams, crouching by their fire in the dawn on the field of Agincourt, had to be got off stage before the king's soliloquy. The chord, the simultaneous striking of several notes, which harmonize and produce a combined effect, is possible only for the novelist. He can count on his readers to catch impressions which would be missed on the stage.

He can, as the dramatist cannot, achieve effects which depend upon understatement. This Homer often does, especially at two great moments which answer one another in the general design of the story. The first is in the quiet, equable, matter-of-fact answer which Odysseus gives to Calypso's offer of immortality. He makes no attempt to explain his

choice; to explain to a Goddess why he prefers
to be a man would have been rather dangerous,
as she knew well enough when she made the
offer. Man's claim to equality with the gods, by
virtue of a field of experience unknown to
them, is implicit in much classical literature;
Aeschylus was the first to utter it, at a period
when men feared the gods less than they did
in the Homeric age. Nimble witted Odysseus
avoids this trap:

'My lady Goddess, I beg you not to resent my
feelings. I too know well enough that my wise
Penelope's looks and stature are insignificant
compared with yours. For she is mortal, while
you have immortality and unfading youth.
Nevertheless I long to reach my home and see
the happy day of my return. It is my never-
failing wish. And what if the powers above do
wreck me out of the wine dark sea? I have a
heart that is inured to suffering and I shall
steel it to endure that too. For in my day I have
had many bitter and shattering experiences in
war and on the stormy seas. So let this new
disaster come. It only makes one more.'

He says this after a demonstration, by
Calypso, of the shortcomings of a goddess. She
has used the language of the heart, having
none; she declares that she knows what pity is,

and that it is only fair to warn him of the boundless miseries which await him if he refuses her offer. Yet she knows perfectly well that he is destined to reach his home in safety, for Hermes has just told her so.

The answering great moment comes with the stringing of the bow. If anybody else proves able to do this, Odysseus' plan miscarries. Had all turned entirely upon this point, as it probably did in the original story, the solution of his predicament, the proof of his right to a place among the living, would have tilted a little too much towards the fairy tale; it would have been of a piece with Cinderella's glass slipper. It will not do for a situation as human and poignant as that which has, by now, been built up. Homer again sticks to the old convention and gives it a new twist. Odysseus is *not* the only man in the world who can string that bow. Telemachus could have done it. Taking his turn, at a fourth try, the young man is just about to succeed when he catches his father's eye and desists. The understatement is masterly. It would never do on the stage; any urgent gesture or appeal from Odysseus would spoil all. By desisting, the young man makes a place for his father, and the fairy-tale element is dismissed.

Had Odysseus refused immortality, risked so

much, and reached home only to be ousted by his son, that choice of mortality would have been imbecile. Men make sacrifices, they bear a love to one another, beyond what they offer to the gods. They know therefore, in their brief and wretched lives, moments of felicity hidden from the Immortals. It was to such a moment, such a son, that Odysseus longed to return.

The story is full of surprises and they are the surprises of great narrative. They are not the purely unexpected, not the sudden turn of fortune, not Habrokomes floating down the Nile. They bring with them an element of recognition and a sense of something already half perceived. Of course! thinks the reader. It must have been so. I should have known it.

Penelope and Odysseus, between them, work up a surprise of this kind. Early in the story the reader has looked forward to their reunion, expecting a tender scene: tears, smiles, exclamations, and embraces. As the story proceeds it becomes clear that this would be an anti-climax. Something else would suit better, for this strange pair. Why does he treat her as he does? Why does he keep his return a secret from her, never a dropping hint at their first interview? He could not have doubted her loyalty, her wit, or her self command. Yet he

194

lets her sob her heart out, after many people—
Telemachus, the swineherd, the cowman, the
nurse, even the dog—know that he has come
home. She is the last person in the house to
learn of it. He will not allow her to know anything until the great fight is over and the hall
is cleaned up again.

Very composedly does she pay him out for all
this when she does know. How, she inquires,
can she be sure that he is not some god in disguise? It would be just like a god to carry on like
this, but . . . a husband? Is this the behaviour
of a husband?

On either side of their hearth these magnificent creatures sit, eyeing one another like
opponents. They are altogether too much for
their son. Telemachus is an admirable young
man but a little conventional, a little over
anxious to do the right thing. These sons of the
great heroes had no easy time of it, although
he came off better than did Orestes or Hip-
polytus. The heroic age was ending and the
stature of mankind was dwindling. It was un-
likely that these young men would ever be able
to do exactly what they chose, as their fathers
had done. They were, rather, engaged with
problems of conduct and with unpleasant duties
which might not have been quite so onerous if

their fathers had not been such unconscionable old ruffians. Telemachus, impeccably filial, does occasionally give the impression that he finds some compensation in regarding himself as, so to speak, an Etonian, which his father emphatically was not. The good youth has just been conscientiously hanging the maids, although not told to do so, and going about it with the more zest because his mother would never let him have anything to do with them. He wants to round off this happy occasion with a conventional family reunion, and he upbraids his mother for not behaving like a womanly woman. His father promptly tells him to make himself scarce; it is not for him, at this time of day, to explain his parents to one another.

Odysseus has already told Nausicaa that the secret of a happy marriage, of a man and woman like-minded keeping house together, is something known only to themselves. He and Penelope are extremely like-minded. She is almost as formidable, almost as nimble-witted, as he is, and she has a pretty hard heart. Her feeling for him is the only thing which can cloud her wits; old tramps with travellers' tales, pretending to bring news of him, can sometimes impose on her. The bond between her and her lord is not a tender one. It is not a case of: *She loved me for the dangers I had passed: and I loved her that she did pity them.* Nausicaa, hearing of those dangers in her father's hall, may have loved him for that reason; she was not the woman for Odysseus, who never asked pity of anybody. Pity would never have moved Penelope. She loves him because he is the only man in the world who can frighten her a little, and can keep her wondering what he will be up to next. He loves her because, to be lord of her, he must use, to the last inch, his nimble wits. That is their secret. There has to be a little skirmish, a battle of wits about a bed, in which he scores, before she falls weeping upon his neck.

The strangest, the most revealing surprise of all comes in the shape of an answer to his prayer, when he stands in his doorway in the dawn, longing for some voice of the living to call him back. The voice which then calls is not an expected voice; it is not a cry from wife or son, not even from the old nurse. It is nameless, the voice of the house itself, going to rack and ruin for want of a master, uncared for, untended, since he went away. There have been other great houses in the story. In the account of them stress has always been laid on the good rule, the order, the management, the cleanliness, the burnishing, the polishing, the thrift, the good husbandry, the efficient servants, each proud of his appointed task, the stately hospitality. So it was in the halls of Menelaus and Alcinous, but not in Ithaca. There all is waste and disorder; the bad servants tyrannize over the good; the guests throw the furniture about; the giggling maids scurry out at night to their lovers. This house, a tavern now rather than a palace, cries out for its lord. An old slave woman, who has been grinding corn all night, raises her plaint:

'Zeus, lord of heaven and earth, what thunder from a starry sky! And never a cloud in sight! You *must* have meant it for some lucky man. Listen to poor me too, and let my wish come true. Here 'tis. Let this very day see the end of these junketings in the Palace. Terrible work this, grinding meal for the young lords. They've broken my back. May this be their last dinner, say I.'

This impersonal voice—poor Me with a breaking back—is the one voice which can, with authority, call the wanderer home.

It is now thirty years since Mr. Forster suggested a view of the novel which still largely prevails. He said roundly that he 'fears and detests' readers who demand a good story, that the story is a 'low atavistic form', a regrettable necessity in the novel, upon which a good writer should rely as little as possible. True merit resides in the comment which he offers upon the events narrated.

Scrutiny of the Odyssey must inevitably suggest an opposing scale of values. Is not comment a regrettable necessity? Are not most writers forced upon it because they lack the power to tell a story? Since they thus depend on it, in order to make their points and evoke their responses, they do well to make it as original, striking and attractive as they can; but do they not reach their finest level, as artists, when they can contrive to dispense with it? Is it not the highest praise of all to say that 'Mr. Homer can tell a story'?

If so, those readers who demand a good story may well be feared and detested. They ask for something which only one out of a million novelists can supply; it is a mercy that so many are willing to be fobbed off with comment.

CHAPTER XIII

The Goosefeather Bed

The fiction-reading public is no longer scolded
for frivolous waste of time. On the contrary it
is, week in week out, urged to accept Reproofs,
note Salutary Reminders, hearken to Timely
Warnings, and swallow Cathartics. Old-
fashioned readers are sometimes quite frightened by such forbidding recommendations. It is
difficult to persuade them that these black
draughts are often both amusing and reward-
ing; that Kafka's *The Castle* is really very
funny; that Mr. Angus Wilson's stories are
called Reproofs, because no reviewer likes to
praise a novelist just now, without including
some certificate for his civic conscience. Mr.
Somerset Maugham, in an interview published
by *The Observer* (November 10th, 1957), re-

marked that Mr. Wilson has 'the traditional virtues of a novelist'. That is why Mr. Wilson has a public, but Mr. Philip Toynbee, anxious for his good name, hastened to point out that 'his fiction is certainly informed by a great deal of moral indignation'.

Old-fashioned readers are not the only rebels. The vogue for admonitory novels can provoke to a certain amount of indignation, less exalted in quality, the kind of reader who likes his edification undiluted, in the form of philosophy, theology, ethics, history, and biography. This stiff-necked type, who often possesses a high intelligence quotient, persists in thinking that a novelist is more respectably employed when delighting a Plato than when dosing a dunce. He snorts at black draughts and reserves his patronage for those down-at-heel descendants of Homer who keep upon the shelf labelled *Crime, Westerns, and Thrillers.* This would have disappointed the early champions of the novel. Some loss of popularity among readers of low intellectual calibre was expected; intransigence among the quick witted was not.

Across the floor, in those aristocratic quarters known as *General Fiction*, there are symptoms of uneasiness. Some writers there are as perverse as the lady in the ballad, who preferred

the cold open field, and Gipsy Geordie, to a
goosefeather bed with a new wedded lord in it.
They wonder if the novel did not fare better
in the old days, when all shared a common
Alsatia. A good many of them believe that their
claim to a footing on Parnassus has been con-
siderably shaken, during the past ten years,
by the appearance of a new critical term: *the
serious novelist.*

This expression began to be used, in about
1947, by people who believed it vital that a
distinction should be drawn between novels
written for commercial purposes and novels
written for other purposes. Many critics have
never adopted this method of indicating
whether, and in what degree, a novel can be
taken seriously. Others place great reliance on
it. Opinions differ so sharply that the objections
of those who dislike the term merit some
scrutiny. They believe that it has fostered
regimentation, and vitiated criticism, by con-
fusing three very different kinds of seriousness:
that of a writer who acknowledges a duty to the
public; that of a writer who acknowledges no
duty save to his subject; seriousness in the
Aristotelian sense—a rare attribute of great
art, evoking an exalted response.

Purposes, other than commercial, for which

a novel can be written are manifold. A short list might include propaganda, edification, creative satisfaction, exhibitionism, malice, a safety valve, and a lark. Any comprehensive label must be a menace if it confers prestige. There are bound to be competing claims for a monopoly of this prestige, by writers and critics who support the superiority of one particular purpose, and who dismiss to the commercial market all who profess any other.

The fatuity of Mr. Clarke, the royal librarian who advised Jane Austen to write 'an historical romance illustrative of the august House of Cobourg' is one of the standing jokes of literature, since her purpose is recognized as incompatible with prescription. That the serious novelist is now expected to disclaim her purpose may be concluded from the fact that his patrons continually prescribe for him. They do so without raising laughter and without eliciting from him the merry but firm reply which Miss Austen gave to Mr. Clarke. Evidence of the measure in which regimentation is now taken for granted was furnished by *The Observer*, in a series of literary interviews published in the Autumn of 1957.

What aims, asked Mr. John Wain of Mr. Lionel Trilling, can a serious novelist legiti-

203

mately propose to himself? Ought his attitudes and ideas to be humane? What subjects does he choose? (September 29th.) These inquiries, advanced in so public a manner, went far to establish certain conclusions: that the serious novel is no work of unfettered imagination; that it is a civic commodity put together upon a sponsored assembly belt; that some occult legislation has taken place rendering some aims legitimate and invalidating others.

It was with relief that many writers, on both sides of the Atlantic, learnt of Mr. Edmund Wilson's stand for liberty. (November 3rd.) He disconcerted Mr. Wain by refusing flatly to endorse any Act of Uniformity against their colleagues. Whenever he was asked what 'the writer' should say, he tiresomely replied: *What writer?* He persisted in thinking, so Mr. Wain complained, that every writer is an 'individual case'.

The assembly-belt critic is no novelty, and he has often, in the past, sung a dirge for the literature which he subjected to *peine forte et dure*. Lamentation over the novel is now sometimes heard from people who continue to prescribe for it with unruffled assurance. Consistency must allow the coveted label to any pretentious and illiterate writer who selects the recommended subjects, professes the legitimate aims, and strikes the orthodox attitudes. The blame for sad stuff must be put upon the novel itself, which is clearly on its last legs if serious novelists cannot be taken seriously. Nor can any commercial writer be forbidden to peddle prescriptions which have won popular favour. Some safeguard, some variant indicating actual merit, had to be found. Before 1947 it was possible to talk about a good novelist, but of this expression many patrons of seriousness are inclined to fight shy. It might entail the labour of identifying and defining the good; this is spared to those whose criterion turns upon intention rather than performance. Lessing, Coleridge, Saint Beuve, and Saintsbury, have all pointed out that the questions put by a capable critic: What has the writer done? Is it good? are far harder to answer than those in which the incompetent take refuge: What did he propose to do? Was it correct? A safe compromise was however discovered and introduced a couple of years ago: *The serious novelist in the best sense.*

This periphrasis can be thrust upon any writer, whether he likes it or not. He may suffer for it if he is young, talented, and original. Assembly-belt sponsors, claiming him as a creditable exhibit, hold him up as a good example to all the serious novelists in the worst sense. The public is assured that he has been up to nothing shady in the commercial line. He is described as 'artistic', praised for knowing the difference between *scare* and *scarify*, and congratulated on the trouble that he has taken to write well. These are thoroughly nasty things to say about an artist. The critic who talks like a governess is always likely to present him as high minded, low-spirited, painstaking, and a bore.

A perfect illustration of this extinguishing eulogy was provided on November 1st, 1957, by one of the disembodied Mr. Clarkes who review for *The Times Literary Supplement*. Two young writers were described as 'most interesting' and serious 'in the best sense' because they are 'deeply concerned to mould their writings into artistic and not merely commercial shapes', and have 'conscientiously' developed their prose styles. Such a preamble might have been less deadly, in spite of its impertinence, had it been followed by praise of their performance; their books were benevolently dismissed as 'disappointing'. The main ingredient in this cup of cold poison is a manifest dislike of art, which tends to smother that unruly element with cautious verbiage. Artistic shapes may sound dismal, but they are not likely to cause trouble on an assembly-belt, and do not smack of the 'individual case'. There is no tribute to any original quality or individual flavour. No evidence is offered, in support of the statement that these are interesting writers, beyond a testimonial to conscientiousness and deep concern. We are merely assured that the victims are doing their best. As much might be said for innumerable writers, including some very bad ones. A Mr. Clarke who can venture no further than this, for people whom he acclaims as highly serious, must live in terror lest literature should break out of its kennel and bite him.

Timidity is but one of the evils bred by reliance on this slip-shod jargon. The exploitation of any grave word, valuable in its proper context, will deplete the resources of criticism. Seriousness in the *best* sense used formerly to convey a particular meaning. It was never treated as a basis for conduct marks to good boys. It paid some recognition to Aristotle's *spoudaiotes*, and to Matthew Arnold's discussion of that sublime quality. When perceived, in any work, it was praised with all the warmth and clarity that a critic could command. If the novel is indeed a form of art, a novel might occasionally display it, rare though it is. That a term, once so impressive, should be thus cheapened and diminished indicates a miserable decline in critical standards.

Whatever the jargon may have signified, ten years ago, it has now been appropriated by a single group in support of a single purpose. Hence the black-draught commendations, so puzzling to old-fashioned readers, which seldom have much reference to the book, the writer, or his purpose. They are only genuinely applicable to one type of writer—the civic novelist, who has pretty well won the competition for a monopoly of seriousness. There can be no comprehensive label for all those who disclaim him as their representative. It will be enough to say, in this context, that a large group of them might be described as outlaws, since they will never allow that the novel can be subjected to legislation. If some Star Chamber has been set up, they never heard of it, and will have none of it. They acknowledge but one decree: *What you can do you may do.* In this, and in many other respects, they are directly opposed to the civic novelist.

He asks what subject he ought to select. In Jane Austen's shoes he would have weighed the importance of *Emma* against that of the House of Cobourg. His object is to edify, to warn, to reprove, to instruct, to rouse the public conscience, and to disseminate valuable ideas. A hundred years ago these ideas were generally religious. Today they are mostly political and social.

The outlaw is unhappy if his subject has not chosen him. He attaches no importance, either to *Emma* or to the House of Cobourg, beyond that with which an author can invest them. His purpose is so to present his imagined thing that the reader will recognize truth in it.

In this he shares the purpose of an artist, but he has no right to claim, for his group, a monopoly of art. The artist can turn up anywhere, under any label. An exceptionally gifted writer, exalted by passion and humility to the level which can reconcile art with didacticism, may turn up among the civics. He has done so in the past, but he is a rare creature, and the civics have always been a numerous tribe. A higher percentage of artists might reasonably be expected among the outlaws, since they have no motive for accepting tasks beyond their capacities.

The civic's dread of commercialism is natural, since the commercial writer is an expert thief of other people's thunder. Should moral indignation promise royalties he will display it, with alarming competence, thus bringing the intentions of his betters into disrepute. In the middle of the last century the market was flooded with religious commercials. It is for this reason that a civic-minded critic will always make a point of mentioning that his protégés have not moulded their writings into commercial shapes. The prolonged hullabaloo over the iniquities and perils of commercialism has had very little bearing on the interests of the novel as a form of art. It is raised on behalf of non-art, which is also non-commercial, and which therefore requires some protective distinction. Art has never stood in need of such anxious chaperonage; the distinction there asserts itself. An artist, to whatever group he belongs, is an individual case. Nobody can steal his thunder, supposing him to have any. A compulsion to write as well as he can may haunt his days and keep him awake at nights; he may lose weight in his efforts to develop his prose style; he knows that this kind of seriousness is shared by very many writers, of all kinds, and he does not expect it to let him in for a public pat on the head. Nor is he likely to slither into commercial shapes by accident.

210

These present no constant and insidious temptation, against which he must be perpetually on his guard. His conscientiousness and deep concern spring from a positive excitement over his subject, and an anxiety to do it justice, rather than from any desperate resolution never, never to misbehave himself. An artistic shape is not a jelly mould into which 'writings' are deliberately crammed at some point on the production line. The ultimate shape of any imaginative work is implicit in its conception, long before a single word has been written. To recognize and obey that compulsive pattern, to rid himself of any too hastily adopted idea of what it ought to be, is one of the labours over which a writer is likely to lose weight. As Charlotte Brontë put it:

'An influence seems to waken . . . which will have its way—putting out of view all behests but its own, dictating certain words and insisting on their being used, whether vehement or measured in their nature . . . rejecting carefully elaborated old ideas, and suddenly creating and adopting new ones.'

It is not the commercial shape which threatens the awakening of this influence so much as a prejudice in favour of some literary convention imposed by the criticism of the moment.

This is often misunderstood by Mr. Clarkes who have perhaps but a slender acquaintance among artists.

Between these groups, the civics and the outlaws, there need be no feud. They might respect one another, provided no confusion arises to invalidate criticism and bewilder the public. Many readers like both types of novel, so long as they know what they are getting. It is the common misfortune of these groups that they must share the great goosefeather bed known as *General Fiction*. There they lie uneasy, each fearing contamination from the other. The civic abhors people who are flippant about commercialism. The outlaw detests people who talk about legitimate aims. Both would be happier if they could, in some way, part company, leaving the civic in undisputed possession of an adjective which he needs for his credit and which is often an insult to the outlaw. Such a dichotomy would benefit their neighbours. Other novelists, writing for other purposes, must find this vendetta among the goosefeathers extremely unsettling.

The main obstacle lies in the difficulty of finding an adequate title for any set of shelves to which the outlaws might retreat. Over that they are something divided. Mr. Maugham, in his *Observer* interview, suggested that Entertainment is a good enough title for any novelist, and asked why people 'are so ashamed of being called entertainers'. Many writers would have replied that it is not shame, which makes them hesitate to accept such a label, so much as a doubt whether readers would recognize it as covering the full range of goods offered. The word suggests a mood of relaxation which would seem to preclude any strenuous pleasure. Entertainment, at one end of the scale, comprises a game of tiddlywinks. Readers might not understand that this simple diversion shares a pigeon hole with the response which they give to some of Mr. Maugham's graver stories. Both are assuredly pleasures, but pleasures of such a very different order. This doubt might be felt by writers who do not for a moment imagine themselves to offer so wide a range as Mr. Maugham.

It could, on the other hand, be argued, that this doubt springs from a fear that readers may be very stupid people. The outlaw, by his own rules, should harbour such a fear as seldom as possible. His best mind imaginable might put Mr. Maugham's value upon entertainment. The label is, but for this one drawback, attractive, since it carries no flavour of edification and will therefore completely distinguish him from the civic. It may, moreover, stimulate him in that task which Henry James considered to be the heaviest known to a novelist: that of imparting to his work 'an agreeable surface'. It is indeed severe labour and it sharpens the perceptions, as do most forms of self-imposed discipline. When engaged on it the writer learns much about the texture of his material and perceives with greater clarity what it is that he *must* say. It toughens that in him which knows no compromise.

This title has another inestimable advantage. It allows complete freedom to all forms of creative activity. No alternative could be suffered which, in an attempt to grade responses, puts creation into a straight waistcoat. This blessing of freedom enabled novelists in the past to write as they pleased, under a label which might be inadequate but which never quenched those who had no mind to be quenched. It never fettered or silenced the giants who won for the novel a home on Parnassus, and to whom it owes liberty and dignity. Only so long as these are preserved can the children of Homer continue in an art which they have brought to mankind from the morning of the world.